Here/Now

Here/Now

Jim Lewis

Jim Lewis

CONTENTS

1. INTRODUCTION — 1
2. MISSISSIPPI CIVIL RIGHTS WORKER (1965-1966) — 4
3. MISSISSIPPI CIVIL RIGHTS LAWYER (1966-1973) — 23
4. NORTH CAROLINA (1974-1977) AND WASHINGTON (1977-1983) — 67
5. SPRINGFIELD (1983-2010) — 84
6. SPRINGFIELD (2010-2022) — 101
7. POEMS — 140
8. PHOTOS — 149
9. DIRECTIONS — 156

INTRODUCTION

NOTE FOR THIS EXPANDED EDITION

Welcome to this edition. I have updated this memoir, to include some recent events and to be more present and personal in my own story.

INTRODUCTION

On July 28, 1940, in New York City, in the afternoon, Mom (Desna) delivers me into this world, and I meet my Dad (Stephen) and my older brother (Steve Jr). When World War II begins, we follow Dad while he serves in the Navy, ordering equipment. After the war, Dad returns to a successful business career, and we move to the New York suburbs.

My life is comfortable, with good schools and summer camps. I read a lot, bike a lot and play sports. In my teen years, I browse through my parents' library and read John Hersey's "The Wall" and "Hiroshima," about life and death in the Warsaw Ghetto during the Holocaust and in Hiroshima just before and right after the Atomic Bomb, and I begin to question the world outside my well-protected environment–a world where some people destroy others. In high school, I write a paper that compares the love and caring that many extend to others with the opposites of caring: hate and indifference. Then in my senior year, I write a 20-page research paper about conformity, asking the basic question in David Riesman's "The Lonely Crowd:" are we independent and "hardened for voyages" or dependent and "softened for encounters?"

In 1958, I finish high school and head off to an Ivy League college (Yale). I begin with science and laboratory courses, thinking of becoming a doctor/psychiatrist, but these courses separate the merely curious–like me–from the serious scientists. So I wander into other courses, uncertain about my interests.

I take a seminar on Greek thought, where we conclude that the Greeks would describe Yale as a place to postpone our entry into the real and often messy world. In this seminar, I write a paper, "Fate, Sin and Circumstance," discussing a play that asks three questions about human existence: do the gods ordain what will happen; do our transgressions, large and small, determine the course of our lives; or is life simply random? Amid these questions, I wonder about the role of human choice.

In 1962, I finish college, determined to choose my own course. I move to New York City and arrange to teach at a private elementary school on Staten Island. In the evenings, I volunteer at Henry Street Settlement House, which serves generations of immigrants on the lower East Side. I work with young people who come to the Settlement House, attempting to get through their teen years without gang affiliation, and I meet their parents, hard-working people who live in public housing complexes, raising large families. I become uncomfortable with being "comfortable," and I begin to commit to social justice.

Can I combine social justice with law school? In 1963, I apply to the law school at the University of Chicago, and enroll there in the fall.

2

MISSISSIPPI CIVIL RIGHTS WORKER (1965-1966)

CHAPTER 1.

In law school, I learn "the legal method:" define the question, analyze the facts and law, and provide an answer. I get an A in the basic course–Elements. And I begin to realize that law school courses do not address social justice, so I become restless and uncomfortable.

In the summer of 1964, known as "Freedom Summer," the southern civil rights movement begins to welcome northern volunteers. These volunteers bring national attention, particularly when three civil rights workers—James Chaney from Mississippi and Michael Schwerner and Andrew Goodman from New York—are murdered by the Klan, with law enforcement assistance, in Neshoba County, Mississippi. By fall 1964, I decide to take three months off from law school, in order to go south and work within the civil rights movement. I want to participate, instead of watching from the sidelines.

I have a friend, Chuck McDew, with several years' experience in civil rights work across the south with the Student Non-Violent Coordinating Committee (SNCC). I ask Chuck to recommend the worst community within the worst state for civil rights, and Chuck suggests McComb, Mississippi, based on his own experience there in 1961 and 1964. I connect with the National Council of Churches in New York, volunteer for their Delta Ministry, fly to New Orleans, take a bus to McComb, and arrive on January 25, 1965.

At the bus station, I meet Reverend Harry J. Bowie from the Delta Ministry. We drive to the Freedom House, to meet my new colleagues. Our project leader is Jesse Harris, a tall, lean SNCC worker, a veteran of years in the struggle. My roommate in the Freedom House is Marshall Ganz, who drops out of Harvard to join the movement and spends most of his time with J.D. Smith at E. W. Steptoe's farm in the county to the west. I meet Karen Pate from Oregon, Ursula Junk from Germany, Loren Cress from Chicago and Dennis Sweeney from California, as well as Roy Lee, a large and gentle man from McComb. These civil rights workers organize within the African American community.

There is white resistance, and it is violent. In the summer of 1964, the Klan bombs seventeen churches and homes in the McComb community, including the Freedom House itself.

I meet local people and try to figure out what I can do to help. I meet Ms. Alyene Quin, owner of the South of the Border Café, located right up the street, and I begin to eat there regularly. Ms. Quin chairs the Pike County Freedom Democratic Party (FDP); the FDP organizes across the state as an alternative to the regular—and segregated—Democratic Party. In the summer of 1964, Ms. Quin's house is bombed. I learn that she and others are invited to Washington, to the White House, to discuss the struggle in Mississippi with President Johnson.

I meet many other voices for the civil rights movement, including Webb Owens, a retired Pullman worker; Ms. Sarah Cotton, who teaches me to play bid whist and to make a tasty and potent drink out of fermented peaches; and Jessie Divens, a young activist. I enjoy meeting people, talking with them, and becoming part of a community–a real community, in the midst of struggle and change.

CHAPTER 2.

Chuck McDew is correct: McComb is an excellent place to participate in the struggle for civil rights. In August 1964, the Pike County FDP joins the FDP across the state in sending a challenge delegation to the National Democratic Convention in Atlantic City. At this Convention, Fannie Lou Hamer speaks for the FDP, telling a national television audience about the all-white Democratic Party's denial of the right of African Americans to register, participate and vote, amid white violence against African Americans across Mississippi. Nonetheless, the Convention denies the FDP challenge and seats the all-white delegation.

In January 1965, the FDP presents a second challenge, this time against the seating of Mississippi's delegation in the United States House of Representatives, because African Americans are denied the opportunity to register, participate and vote all across the state during the November 1964 elections, amid widespread Klan violence. The House of Representatives allows the FDP to take depositions and gather testimony.

I arrive in Mississippi in time to attend depositions at the Pike County courthouse in Magnolia, ten miles south of McComb. At these depositions, I hear testimony about the civil rights struggles in 1961 and 1964: about John Hardy, a SNCC worker who accompanies people trying to register to vote in 1961, and is beaten with a pistol by a voting registrar and then prosecuted for disturbing the peace; about Herbert Lee, active in civil rights, murdered in 1961 in public in cold blood by a state legislator, E. H. Hurst; about a witness to Lee's murder, Louis Allen, himself murdered–apparently by Deputy Sheriff Billy Caston–in early 1964, when Allen prepares to testify. The evidence is clear: almost every African American who applies for voter registration is rejected, and the political system maintains segregation and white supremacy, enforced by white violence–including murder. Despite this evidence, Congress denies the FDP challenge and accepts the Mississippi delegation.

CHAPTER 3.

I meet each weekend with Freedom School students, and I begin to participate. I learn that SNCC begins the first Freedom School in McComb in 1961, when the African American high school expels two students–Brenda Travis and Ike Lewis–for their civil rights activity, and most of the other students walk out in protest. In 1964, this Freedom School reopens, offering an opportunity for young people to read and discuss material that connects to their own experience, like James Baldwin's "The Fire Next Time." These young people are concerned, rightly concerned, about a system that expects them to be segregated and submissive.

The students determine to challenge this system. They decide to go downtown and talk with Police Chief George Guy, who enforces the local system of segregated justice. We prepare and off we go. We sit down with Chief Guy, and the students spell out their expectation: equal treatment and equal justice.

The students also expect that African Americans should have the opportunity to register, participate and vote, and they propose a peaceful protest at the county courthouse. We prepare for this, ensuring that students understand the risk and obtain parental permission, and ensuring that adults and civil rights workers go as well. Then, for two days in late February, fifty of us, students, adults and civil rights workers, protest at the county courthouse, carrying signs, singing freedom songs, complaining that Voting Registrar Glen Fortenberry rejects almost every African American applicant. Our non-violent protest, within this violent corner in this violent state, is a significant statement about the need for peaceful change.

My mind races with the possibility of change. We call this "high on freedom." I share this feeling with Harry Bowie, and he tries to bring me back toward reality. And on our third day, we meet reality. The Mississippi Highway Patrol arrives in force and announces, "You're all under arrest." We kneel–this is the picture on the cover of this book–and they take us away.

The Pike County jail is much too small to hold fifty prisoners, so the Highway Patrol takes us to the Hinds County Jail in Jackson, the state capital. I ride with Harry, and I ask him, for the benefit of the two patrol officers in front, where this struggle is going. I expect Harry to respond with a message about change or humanity or justice. Instead, he simply says, "We must keep pushing. They will keep pushing against us. If we stop, they will win."

At the Hinds County Jail, officers book and photograph us. They ask, "Are you a Communist?" I answer, "No, I am not." They take my possessions and shoes and put me in a cell by myself. I relax and reflect. We don't seek to go to jail, but we realize that the white power structure may put us in jail for a while. I begin to appreciate that a decent person should be prepared to protest and go to jail, when the power structure is not also decent. And I feel free, since I now know that I am willing to act–peacefully–on my belief in social justice, even if this requires jail.

After three days, we are released on bail. We go in together and come out together, even more committed. But first, the civil rights workers decide that three days in jail is worth three days of drinking, so we buy some bootleg alcohol. As it turns out, one afternoon of bootleg alcohol is sufficient, and we return to our work.

CHAPTER 4.

I call Mom and Dad every Sunday, but I couldn't call from jail. I call when we are released from jail, and Mom and Dad decide to come to McComb and see for themselves. A few weeks later, I take a bus down to New Orleans, meet them at the airport, and we drive to McComb.

They stay with Ms. Quin. On Saturday night, we go to a juke joint in the African American community for drinks and some music. Mom and Dad are tired and far from home, the Upper East Side of New York, so they end their evening early. At Ms. Quin's, the phone rings several times that evening. When Mom answers, the caller asks whether Ms. Quin has any "butter," and Mom checks the refrigerator. Mom begins to suspect bootlegging, and asks me the next morning. I explain that home brewing and bootlegging are extremely common, even though a state law forbids all sale of alcohol.

On Sunday, we form a caravan of six cars–Freedom School students, community members, civil rights workers and Mom and Dad–and head out to E. W. Steptoe's farm in the adjacent county, Amite County, for a picnic. J. D. Smith and I go to a little store at a crossroads to buy bread, bologna and soda. When we return, someone mentions to me that the Klan meets at that store.

We have a good day at Steptoe's farm, playing softball, eating, visiting and just relaxing, before we return to McComb. Mom and Dad drive back to New Orleans and fly to New York. They come a long way from their comfortable New York apartment, and they have a chance to see the community, how we live and what we do. They become active supporters of the movement.

CHAPTER 5.

I like being in McComb. I like the people. I'm learning about social justice in the real world. I'm trying to help McComb become part of the America that we expect.

I listen to project leader Jesse Harris. Jesse becomes active in the movement in 1961, and is arrested among hundreds of Freedom Riders when they desegregate the interstate bus station in Jackson, receiving two months of hard time at Parchman Penitentiary. One day, we share a beer–Pabst is cold and inexpensive, and we have little money–and Jesse offers some experience and wisdom about the difference between risk and fear. Risk can be assessed, even the extra risk that comes with civil rights work. Fear involves danger that is beyond assessment and control. For civil rights work, Jesse suggests putting fear aside, and simply deciding whether the specific purpose justifies the specific risk. For example, a man telephones the Freedom House one afternoon, I answer, and the man threatens to bomb us. Jesse takes the phone from me and says, "Don't call. Just surprise us." Jesse does not allow these threats to limit our work. And ever since this civil rights experience, I try to put fear aside, to consider the purpose and the risk, and to continue forward when there is purpose.

Another day, sharing another beer, Jesse talks about the "welcome table," where people can come together and share their individual views. Jesse says that we should all be able to sit at the welcome table–or we should knock the table down. I believe in the welcome table, and I come away determined to establish welcome tables wherever I can.

I also listen to Harry Bowie. He is short, stocky, mixed ethnicity, an ordained Episcopalian, Phi Beta Kappa in college in upstate New York, deeply thoughtful, fearless and completely committed to the struggle. One day, Harry describes the civil rights movement to me as a "process" for local people to find their own voices and expand their opportunities.

Harry is stating the movement's basic principle, "let the local people decide"–it is their life, their community–before we offer support and assistance. I gain respect for this process: be present, engage with people, listen, connect and–if asked–provide some support.

Another day, Harry shares his concern that the civil rights movement will be followed by a violent white reaction, like the white reaction that brings an end to Reconstruction (1866-1876). During Reconstruction, Mississippi and other southern states have federal troops, desegregated voting, desegregated government and the beginning of public education. After the 1876 national election, the federal troops withdraw, the Klan rises, the vote is lost, the schools close, and the white community reasserts total control. Mississippi's last Reconstruction governor predicts that white supremacy will return African Americans to "serfdom," and his prediction proves correct. Most former slaves have no land, so they depend on white landowners for work and subsistence wages. This is Harry's fear: a period with some gains, followed by white reaction and resistance and a return to serfdom.

I also learn from the example set by Roy Lee, a tall, strong and gentle young man. Roy listens to people and cares about what they say. Roy watches out over all of us, and is the person to have with you in any tough spot. From Roy and his example, I learn the most important lesson: be present, listen and care.

While I listen and learn, I also turn to my old friend: independent reading. I read memoirs like Anne Moody's "Coming of Age in Mississippi," histories like Vernon Lane Wharton's book about Reconstruction and Howard Zinn's book about SNCC (with a chapter about SNCC's 1961 effort in McComb), as well as books about Gandhi and non-violence. I become committed to non-violence as a tactic–violence will complicate the effort to move forward–but also as a personal imperative–to do no harm.

If I'm going to continue in Mississippi, I will need to understand the white power structure that controls the entire state. So I read John Dollard's classic sociological study, "Caste and Class in a Southern Town," examining Indianola in the Mississippi Delta in the 1930s. Dollard analyzes the economic, social, sexual, political and educational advantages that the white community obtains through supremacy, segregation and suppression. From this book, as well as my daily experience in McComb, I see how the white community chooses white advantage and African American disadvantage. In McComb and across the state, the white community enforces its advantages and its prejudices. I learn to reject stereotypes and prejudices, and to be more thoughtful about my own judgments.

I continue to listen and learn. Mary King and Casey Hayden of SNCC write an article about the struggle of women within the civil rights movement, and I overhear Karen Pate and Ursula Junk discuss the need for a women's movement. That day, I begin to appreciate more fully how women also struggle for equal opportunity.

One day, walking along a dusty road, I feel how much I like being in Mississippi. I like the people. They matter. Their community has strength, even though the white community imposes limits on this strength.

I like the sense of purpose that comes with this struggle. Can people in Mississippi gain the American promise of genuine economic, political, social and educational opportunity for each and every person, with no limitation based on race, religion, gender, origin, age or belief–with no artificially-imposed limits? This will require hard work. I want–I choose–this work. I hope that I can find a way to do this work.

CHAPTER 6.

After three months in Mississippi, it's April and time to return to law school. I take the train, the "City of New Orleans," back to Chicago. And I seek out my girlfriend, Arden Lang.

I first see Arden in late 1963, when she's with two law students, Larry Schwartz and David Tatel. She's really cute. Could we meet? Yes. In early 1964, Arden comes with David to an appellate court argument at the law school, and we meet and talk. She's fun and engaging. We look for each other at a few parties, but we don't find each other. Finally, I see Arden late one evening at Jimmy's Woodlawn Tap, and we talk. She suggests a ride on my motorcycle, and I agree, delighted. We ride for six hours, crisscrossing the south side of Chicago.

Arden and I like each other. I'm new to this and not good, not attentive, but I'm delighted each time we find each other, and my feelings deepen and deepen. In late 1964, I say to Arden that I'm headed to Mississippi, not sure what will happen, and that she may not hear from me. Yes, I make a big mistake: not communicating.

When I return in April 1965, I seek out Arden, and we talk. She's dating a classmate. I don't offer a commitment. Our relationship comes to an end.

Dear reader, please do not lose heart.

CHAPTER 7.

I'm back in law school, but my heart and mind remain in Mississippi, so I hop on "The City of New Orleans" and return to McComb. A few weeks later, I return to school, finish spring quarter, and take the train to McComb for the summer of 1965.

When I reach McComb, I learn that the FDP is planning a large protest at the state capitol in Jackson, in support of the federal Voting Rights Act. What is the Voting Rights Act?

In March 1965, Dr. Martin Luther King, Jr. of the Southern Christian Leadership Conference (SCLC) and John Lewis of SNCC begin a large voting rights march from Selma, Alabama toward the state capitol in Montgomery. On "Bloody Sunday," March 7, 1965, Alabama law enforcement charges on horseback into the marchers, beating the protestors. This attack is shown on national television news, and this country responds. A federal court orders the state to allow and protect this march, and Congress begins to develop a federal Voting Rights Act.

Why would we protest in Jackson? As Congress works on the Voting Rights Act, the Mississippi legislature meets in order to impose additional restrictions on voting. In response, the FDP organizes a protest. In June, 800 of us begin a march toward the state capitol, and we are all promptly arrested. Leaders and white protestors are taken to the Hinds County jail, but several hundred African American protestors are held in much more difficult conditions, in a fenced area at the state fairground, amid summer heat.

The county jail maintains racial segregation. Our cell has 16 white protestors in eight double-decker bunk beds. A cellmate explains a hunger strike and I decide to do this, but he does not. Jail food is fatback, molasses and grits in the morning, and boiled peas and beans for lunch and dinner; I drink a lot of water and don't miss the food. After 12 days, the Lawyers Constitutional Defense Committee gathers enough bail money for all 800 of us to come out together from the jail and fairgrounds, and I emerge thin, unshaven, dirty, smelly and tired. A friend, Jesse Divens, sees me and screams.

CHAPTER 8.

I head back to McComb, to clean up and begin work. The civil rights movement has formed the largest Head Start program in the country, the Child Development Group of Mississippi (CDGM), with funding from the federal War on Poverty. CDGM opens centers across the entire state, with a white employee for each center. I become a resource teacher in a church south of McComb, and I rent a room nearby from the father of Bo Diddley, the rock and roll legend. I settle into a routine, walking over to the school, spending the day helping in any way that I can, walking home in the evening. The children are energetic and wonderful, and we make sure to involve parents in their child's development.

Mississippi does not require young people to go to school. Our Head Start has one boy, age 9, thin, who has never been to school before. Frightened, he runs away for several days. What should I do about this? If I chase him, this wouldn't help him resolve his fright. Instead, I sit and wait on the church steps, able to watch him as he runs down the dirt road. Each time, he slows and turns around, looks back, sees me waiting, and slowly walks back. I welcome his return. And after a few days, he begins to manage his fear and to participate in class. This haunts me still: age 9, skinny, frightened, no schooling, family not seeing to his education.

We have an enormous advantage, when people care about our education.

As summer ends, students prepare for school. For the first time, African American high school students are permitted to choose the white high school, in order to begin a limited form of desegregation–"freedom-of-choice"–that enables the school district to maintain federal education funding. I seriously consider staying in McComb and teaching, in order to help with the desegregation process, so I speak with the local school superintendent and the state teacher accreditation agency, but I decide that I would be more helpful as a civil rights lawyer.

I am supposed to drive a few African American students to and from the formerly all-white high school for the first month, before I return to law school, but I miss the first day because of my third arrest. On the Sunday before school begins, a small group, including myself, Ms. Quin and her son Anthony, go to Percy Quin State Park and swim in the lake. We've tried the park before, but we've been chased away by white people with firecrackers and bricks. This Sunday, the park is officially closed and we are alone, until a ranger shows up, points a gun at us, arrests us, and takes us to the county jail. Our cell is a square concrete room with concrete beds and a hole in the floor, serving as a toilet. After one night, we are released on bond.

For the next month, I drive five students–Marionette Travis, Thelma and Vernell Eubanks, Barbara Lee and one other–to and from the high school. We talk in the morning, but the students become quiet when we cross the invisible line into the white community, and we talk in the afternoon, once we cross the invisible line out of the white community. It's not easy for the students to desegregate a formerly-white school, but they complete the year successfully and even make a few friends. I'd like to know more about their experience, but I have to leave in October 1965, for my final year of law school.

CHAPTER 9.

I read my law books, go to classes, pass my exams, and approach the finish line at law school. It's time to look for work. I want to work at only one place, the Lawyers Constitutional Defense Committee (LCDC) in Jackson, so I hand-write a one-page letter to Al Bronstein at LCDC, and he offers me a job starting in September 1966, at $150 per month, with a car allowance and a free room at the house that LCDC maintains for volunteers. I am delighted. The civil rights movement needs legal support, and LCDC does great work for us each time we are arrested.

In June 1966, I graduate and go for a military physical; they reject me, because I'm out on bail. So I get in my car, drive to Mississippi, and connect up with the "Meredith March" at Tougaloo College, a private and predominantly

African American college that is a few miles north of Jackson. This Meredith March starts when James Meredith–who desegregates the University of Mississippi, "Ole Miss," in 1962– begins a one-person "March Against Fear" from Memphis to Jackson. As soon as he crosses into Mississippi, a white sniper shoots him in the back, seriously wounding him. SCLC and SNCC come together to complete this march, bringing the civil rights movement to town after town along the way. I arrive at Tougaloo in time to hear Stokely Carmichael, the new head of SNCC, speak about the need for "Black Power." The next day, the march completes the final miles into Jackson for a big rally, about 15,000 people, at the state capital. Instead of marching, I reconnect with friends to share a few beers and talk. I've made mistakes in my days, and it is a mistake to miss the conclusion of this historic march.

I head back to McComb, until it's time to start at LCDC. I stay at Ms. Quin's house, and get to know her children, Caroline, Jackie and Anthony, much better. Caroline is a young adult, intelligent, talented and nice. Jackie is a young girl, also intelligent, talented and nice. And Anthony is a wonderful young person, age 7, cute, intelligent, energetic, funny. He's been through a lot. His house is bombed in 1964; he is arrested with his Mother in the 1965 protest in Jackson; and he is arrested again when we swim at Percy Quin State Park. Anthony and I become close friends, even brothers, as we will see.

CHAPTER 10.

I am truly grateful for my friends in McComb. They help me learn how to become the decent and useful person that I wish to be, within the real world.

What is the real world? It's a complicated place, but my time in McComb helps me find three common threads:

First, each person is individual, just as I am, mixing what you might expect with what surprises you; I learn to appreciate the expected and the surprises.

Second, individuals come together to form communities, and these communities develop characteristics; I learn from experience that the primary characteristic of the communities across Mississippi is a white power structure that imposes injustice–political, economic, educational and social injustice–that is based on race; and I'd like to help change this.

And third, the local communities, African American and white, have to change individual expectations and struggle toward social justice, and I'd like to be part of these struggling communities and work with others to bring about this change.

It's September 1966, and it's time to drive 80 miles up to Jackson, move my few belongings into the LCDC house, and begin work with LCDC.

3

MISSISSIPPI CIVIL RIGHTS LAWYER (1966-1973)

CHAPTER 1.

When I start with LCDC, I know very little about actually practicing law. In law school, we focus on legal theory. The school's unofficial motto is, "That may work in the real world, but will it work in theory?" And I don't work in a law office in the summers of 1964 or 1965, so practicing law is new to me.

When I begin work, Al Bronstein asks me to prepare a legal complaint to strike down a state statute. I respond with the most basic question, "What is a legal complaint?" This doesn't give him confidence, so he prepares the complaint himself.

Al is short, stocky and fearless, like Harry Bowie. He comes from New York to Mississippi in the summer of 1964, and quickly becomes a primary source of legal support for the civil rights movement across the state. He ensures that movement people get out of jail and get a defense, and he also takes on the state's political system and its misallocation of power. He is an extraordinary leader.

At LCDC, we get threatening calls from time to time. We have a listed phone number at the LCDC house, so I receive these threatening calls. I listen to see whether there's actual and imminent danger, then I hang up. If the threat is particularly creative, I call Al and pass on the threat. We don't slow down for these threats, because we have work to do.

CHAPTER 2.

Al analyzes the new Voting Rights Act, together with Lawrence Guyot, Chair of the Mississippi FDP. In 1890, Mississippi establishes a "constitutional interpretation" test for voter registration. In county-by-county litigation in the 1960s, the United States Department of Justice proves that every voting registrar uses this constitutional interpretation test to accept almost every white applicant and reject almost every African American applicant, in order to maintain white political control. The Voting Rights Act eliminates this constitituional interpretation test and its discretionary and discriminatory application, so that African American applicants have a legitimate opportunity to register. Across the state, voter registration promptly jumps up from about 5% to about 60% within the African American community. This desegregates the political system as well as the jury system, since juries come from lists of registered voters.

Al and Guyot focus on Sections 4 and 5 of the Voting Rights Act, saying that states and localities with a history of racial discrimination cannot put a new voting law into effect unless the state or locality submits the proposed change to the United States Department of Justice for review, and the Department concludes that the change is not intended to discriminate. When Al asks me to prepare the legal complaint–and I respond, "What is a legal complaint?"– LCDC and the FDP seek to strike down one of the state statutes that the Mississippi legislature passes in the summer of 1965. Al prepares and files the complaint; the case works its way up to the United States Supreme Court, and is combined for argument with other Voting Rights Act cases; and the Supreme Court decides that states with a history of discrimination cannot enforce new voting laws without review and clearance from the Department of Justice. Allen v. Virginia State Board of Elections, 393 U.S. 544 (1969).

This invalidates Mississippi's new voting law, and this provides a small and belated measure of justice for the 800 of us who protest this new voting law, spending twelve days in the county jail or the state fairgrounds in June 1965.

CHAPTER 3.

I try to learn the practice of law as fast as I can, and to get ready for the Mississippi bar exam in mid-1967. Until I pass this exam, I work on voting matters outside the courtroom. In summer 1967, the FDP prepares candidates for November general elections, the first since the Voting Rights Act. I prepare workbooks for each office–sheriff, constable, tax collector, county supervisor–showing the powers of the office. Guyot, Harry Bowie and I meet with candidates for these offices, in week-long sessions at four locations across the state. Guyot and Harry teach how to organize and run an effective campaign, and I teach the potential of each office.

I also work to ensure integrity in the voting process. For example, there is a primary in summer 1967 in Marshall County, with a close race for a place on the general election ballot. The African American candidate for sheriff, Skip Robinson, asks for my help at the official recount. I sit right next to the county clerk as he reads the paper ballots, and I see that he often ignores Skip's name and instead calls a vote for his opponent. I challenge each misreading. After about an hour, the election officials recess and talk to the clerk, he improves his reading, and Skip gets onto the November ballot, but he loses in the general election.

For the November 1967 general election, I write and distribute a workbook for FDP poll-watchers, explaining the entire practice and procedure for voting: eligibility, voter assistance, challenging, counting. FDP candidates have local people to poll-watch, and 300 additional poll-watchers arrive from out of state. I provide the workbook and training for the 300 from out of state, before the FDP sends them out to their assigned community.

On election day, we stand by the phones in the event of trouble. That evening, I get a call that a poll-watcher is in trouble, so I go with David Barnum, a Tougaloo professor who rooms at the LCDC house, to a rural polling place north of Canton. We find an African American law student with a jacket, tie and briefcase, closely watching the vote count, just as I had done for Skip Robinson. It's dark and getting late; the polling place is rural and isolated; there are forty pick-up trucks outside with gun racks; and there are forty unhappy white men inside the crowded polling place. I suggest to the student that he leave with us. He wants to stay, since the vote count is close and not yet final. I suggest again that he leave with us, and he reluctantly agrees. His candidate, David Johnson, loses by five votes, and we file a court challenge that is not successful.

Years later, the student, now a lawyer and friend, tells me that he had a gun in his briefcase for protection that night. I reply, "You were outnumbered and outgunned."

In these November 1967 elections, the poll-watchers all get home safely, and the FDP has some success. A dozen African American candidates win local offices, and one African

American, Robert Clark of Holmes County, wins a race for the state legislature.

Robert Clark defeats a white incumbent, who challenges the election and hires Charles Clark, Mississippi's most-experienced election lawyer and later Chief Judge of the United States Court of Appeals, to question Robert Clark's election. Dick Sobol of LCDC and I–I pass the bar exam and get my law license in mid-1967–represent Robert Clark in a deposition at the Holmes County Courthouse in Lexington. Charles Clark questions Robert Clark at length, but cannot find any flaw in his eligibility or election. Finally, Charles Clark starts to ask about groups that Robert Clark might belong to and groups that might support him, in an effort to try to establish some "guilt by association." I ask for a recess. The United States Supreme Court has already considered several cases in which southern states seek to find out group memberships and intimidate group members, and we advise Robert Clark to refuse to answer on grounds that the Supreme Court has determined that the privacy of group membership is protected by the Constitution. We assert our objection, and the deposition ends.

As the legislature approaches its opening in January 1968, we still do not know whether they will seat Robert Clark. We prepare for a struggle, but the legislature drops the challenge at the last minute and swears him in. To fast forward, he goes on to serve many years with distinction, and when he retires, his son wins his position. As years go by, many other African

Americans win election to local and county offices, as well as the State House, State Senate and the Mississippi Supreme Court.

I see Robert Clark most recently in 2014, when a documentary, "Dirt and Deeds in Mississippi," including interviews with both of us, is previewed in Jackson. He is well, and we are truly delighted to see each other again.

CHAPTER 4.

In early 1967, before I pass the bar exam, Al sends me to Carroll County to observe a case brought by a civil rights worker and some local people against a café owner. When I arrive at the courthouse, there is already a defense attorney and a jury of four white men and two African American men, but no county attorney. The defense attorney asks me to do more than observe, to actually prosecute the case, and I foolishly accept. I don't yet have a license. Yes, bad choice.

I ask the civil rights worker and local people to tell their story: they go in to desegregate the café, the owner chases them out with a gun, and the owner then follows their car down the road shooting at them. There is no cross examination, no defense and no argument. The jury retires to the jury room for a few minutes, then comes out and says, "We have a verdict but we don't know how to spell it." I suggest that they just do their best, and they retire again and emerge again, this time with a scrap of paper that says "Not g." This is as much as the six jurors can spell. Several months later, I hear that the café owner runs for sheriff and wins.

CHAPTER 5.

Once I gain my law license, I begin to help Alfred Windom. He is serving a life sentence for "attempted rape" in 1961, based on an allegation that he touched his white female employer improperly. Windom is arrested the day of the alleged event, taken immediately to court, meets with an appointed lawyer for fifteen minutes, promptly pleads guilty, gets the maximum sentence–life–and goes straight to prison. No one ever slows down to look at the facts.

This is swift–but not justice. No African American has served on a grand jury or trial jury in the county in anyone's memory, despite 80 years of United States Supreme Court rulings that jury segregation invalidates the entire process of criminal justice. I file a federal case and take the court-appointed defense lawyer's deposition; he acknowledges that no white lawyer ever challenges jury segregation and that fifteen minutes of legal representation does not allow sufficient time to look into the case. This defense lawyer also says that he does not know that in 1959, in the adjacent county, an African American lawyer, R. Jess Brown from Jackson, later a colleague with LCDC, does challenge jury segregation, and that Jess Brown's client, Mack Charles Parker, is promptly taken from jail, killed and thrown into the river. When Alfred Windom is arrested in 1961, he knows about Mack Charles

Parker and wants to get away from the area as quickly as possible, even to Parchman Penitentiary.

The state takes Windom's deposition, and he says that he never has a lawyer. For this statement, the state indicts Windom for perjury. We point out to the state judge that perjury in a federal deposition may be a federal offense but cannot be a state offense, and the state judge dismisses the indictment.

Then the federal court invalidates Windom's conviction, based on jury discrimination. The court allows the state to try Windom properly, but the state does not wish to try him, so the penitentiary puts him on a bus to Jackson. I meet Windom at the bus station and take him to stay the night in the LCDC house. The next day, I take him to a plane for Detroit, where family waits to help him. The state appeals, and the federal Court of Appeals agrees that the conviction is invalid, because fifteen minutes with a lawyer is insufficient representation and defense. Windom v. Cook, 423 F.2d 721 (5th Cir. 1970).

For LCDC, I work on six cases for young people in the state juvenile institution. In each case, I obtain the juvenile's prompt release. I also represent a young man, age 13, African American, from Madison County, charged with making inappropriate calls to a young white woman whose father happens to be a law enforcement officer. The sheriff, a large and intimidating man, traces the call to a specific phone, arrives at the address, talks to six young men there, and takes this young man for further interrogation at the sheriff's office, leading to a confession late at night.

The African American community is genuinely concerned about this young man. They invite me to a mass meeting of about 300 people, and ask me to take this case. I begin immediately, and find that the county has the young man, small and frightened, in an isolation cell in the adult jail, because they have no other place for a juvenile. I have to get him out of this isolation cell, before it destroys this young man's spirit. I go to state court for release, without success, and then to federal court. The federal judge says that he doesn't have time to consider the matter. I respond that we'll appeal immediately to the Court of Appeals, and that I'd like release pending this appeal. The judge says that I cannot appeal the scheduling of a case and cannot obtain release pending appeal, but the judge does allow me thirty minutes in his law library to find a case allowing what I seek. Thirty minutes later, I have a pile of books. I read case after case to the increasingly angry judge, who then decides that he does in fact have time to hear the case the next day. And at this hearing, the judge concludes that a juvenile has the right to release, similar to an adult, before hearing or trial. I get this young man out of jail and back to his family.

Soon thereafter, we have the juvenile court trial on the charges. I challenge the only significant evidence, a young person's confession late at night in the office of a large and intimidating sheriff. Is this confession voluntary or coerced?

Does the young man, age 13, understand his constitutional rights, as in Miranda v. Arizona? The trial judge decides that the process is lawful, and we appeal, continuing the young man's release. When I file an appellate brief with many federal cases on these issues, the state concedes and drops the charges, ending the matter.

Another day, I'm reading about a new legal theory: that it is unconstitutional to hold people in jail after the end of their sentence, if they cannot pay a fine that is still owed. While I'm reading about this theory, I'm presented with this reality: a woman knocks on our door, enters, and tells me that her son has just completed his six month sentence for burglary, but he is to be held for six more months in order to credit $3 per day to a $500 fine that he cannot pay. I promptly go to state court, without success, and then to federal district court, again without success. The federal judge says that this process treats each person with a fine in the same way, "rich man, poor man, beggar man and thief." And we appeal. Since the appeal may take more than the six months remaining to pay the fine, I move for release pending appeal, to ensure that the final decision will make a difference, and the Court of Appeals orders release. While we wait to argue the appeal, the United States Supreme Court rules in a similar case that a state cannot keep a person in jail after the end of a sentence, to pay a fine. Williams v. Illinois, 399 U.S. 235 (1970). The Court of Appeals follows this Supreme Court ruling. Thames v. Thomas, 433 F.2d 68 (5th Cir. 1970).

I would like this to end the use of jail for people who are unable to pay a fine, a form of "debtor's prison," but I know that this still goes on, one way or another, throughout this country.

And I am haunted by all of this, how we treat our adults, our young people, our poor people, throughout the criminal and juvenile justice system. When we look closely, we find injustice in case after case. Our small office is unable to reach and correct every injustice. There are too many. I am agitated, and I should be.

CHAPTER 6.

Mississippi is the poorest state. The public assistance system, like the criminal justice system, is full of injustice. So I work with welfare rights groups across the state; I write and distribute a question-and-answer workbook, "Your Welfare Rights," that explains the system and the rights that people have; and I represent many individuals in administrative hearings to challenge improper decisions.

I am particularly concerned about the limits on cash benefits. For a single parent with three children and no other income, the maximum possible benefit is $50 per month. In 1966, the Mississippi Chapter of the United States Commission on Civil Rights holds a formal hearing on social welfare in the state; I testify that $50 per month for a family of four, if applied solely toward food, would allow about 14 cents per meal per person throughout a month, and I further testify that this amount would be likely to starve parents and children. After these hearings, we meet in Washington to discuss this with the United States Department of Health, Education and Welfare, but our advocacy does not change the state's failure to provide a survival cash benefit.

There is, however, some change. In 1967, Senator Robert Kennedy comes through the Mississippi Delta, followed by national news organizations, exposing the terrible shortage of food. This stimulates a federal effort, supported by agricultural and urban areas, to expand food programs, leading to a much more effective food stamp program. These food stamps supplement the state's inadequate financial support, the maximum of $50 per month, and these stamps reduce the risk of starvation.

CHAPTER 7.

After the 1967 elections, Al Bronstein leaves to take a leadership position with the Kennedy School of Government at Harvard University. Al receives a MacArthur Foundation "Genius Grant" and establishes and leads the National Prison Project for the American Civil Liberties Union (ACLU). Al comes to Mississippi when he is most needed; he defends those who most need help, including 50 of us arrested in Magnolia and 800 of us arrested in Jackson; he challenges the white power structure that is strangling the state; he gains the respect of all—and he gives me a job and an opportunity.

In early 1968, Armand Derfner arrives to replace Al. Armand is born in Europe, leaves just before the Holocaust, goes to Princeton for college and then to Yale Law School, works for a federal appellate judge and a corporate law firm, then comes to Mississippi to serve the civil rights movement. He is brilliant and empathetic.

Armand asks me to argue Edgar Love's criminal appeal in the Mississippi Supreme Court. Edgar leaves his farm employment and joins the civil rights movement in 1966 when the Meredith March comes through his county; he is charged with stealing farm equipment when he leaves his employment; he is convicted by an all-white jury; and he appeals. I look at the trial record and notice that there is evidence that he and others use this farm equipment while doing farm work a week before the equipment is missing, but no further evidence that he takes anything.

I know that we have two strikes against us–an African American client and an attorney who is not a "good ole boy"–so I prepare thoroughly to ensure that they don't get a third strike past us. At oral argument, I compare Edgar to an automobile mechanic who uses some automobile equipment a week before it is missing, and is later charged with stealing the equipment, with no further evidence. The Mississippi Supreme Court agrees that there is no evidence of a crime, and reverses Edgar's conviction. Love v. State, 208 So.2d 755 (Ms.Sup.Ct. 1968). The Court concludes, "There simply was no accurate, definite, adequate or substantial evidence of any of the essential elements of the offense."

This haunts me too, that an all-white jury will convict an African American at trial, even when there is no evidence that the person commits a crime.

CHAPTER 8.

Soon after I argue Edgar Love's case, I have my first solo trial. Authorities in Leland shoot tear gas at peaceful civil rights protestors, just a few days before a school board election. I file a federal court complaint and subpoena Hodding Carter, publisher of the nearby Greenville newspaper, who is visiting Leland when they tear gas the protestors. Carter gives an eyewitness description of the events, and the court orders the town to allow peaceful demonstrations, without tear gas. And I begin to truly enjoy trial work.

On April 4, 1968, James Earl Ray assassinates Martin Luther King in Memphis. Across America, many cities erupt, including Jackson. My law school roommate and his wife, Peter and Ann Kolker, happen to be visiting this weekend, and it's not safe for us to go anywhere, so we sit on the front porch of the LCDC house and listen to sirens. Within a few days, the New York Times quotes the final paragraph of Dr. King's final speech in Memphis, and I put his words on the wall of my office: "Well, I don't know what will happen now. We've got some difficult days ahead. But it really doesn't matter with me now, because I've been to the mountaintop. And I don't mind. Like anybody, I would like to live a long life. Longevity has its place. But I'm not concerned about that now. I just want to do God's will. And He's allowed me to go up to the mountain. And I've looked over. And I've seen the Promised Land. I may not get there with you. But I want you to know tonight, that we, as a people, will get to the Promised Land! And so I'm happy, tonight. I'm not worried about anything. I'm not fearing any man. Mine eyes have seen the glory of the coming of the Lord."

After the assassination, there are peaceful protests across Mississippi. People in Shelby begin peaceful daytime demonstrations, and the town responds with a broad curfew for adults and young people. Armand and I go to court, and we get the curfew struck down. Fifty people in Holly Springs begin a peaceful voting rights protest, and the sheriff orders a mass arrest. Hours after the arrest, Deputy Sheriff Ray Bright "discovers" evidence of marijuana in the envelopes that contain the possessions of three leaders: Skip Robinson (former candidate for sheriff), R. B. Cottonreeder from SCLC, and the minister of the largest African American church.

Then the state court judge, the prosecutor and the sheriff decide to arrest Armand and myself. When I finish arguing a pretrial motion in state court in the marijuana cases, Armand comes forward from the audience to listen to the judge's decision, and he is arrested because he is not licensed in Mississippi and the judge will not allow him to listen in the area reserved for lawyers–this is perhaps "listening without a license." We get him out on bail.

When the state court judge sets the marijuana cases for trial, we remove these cases to federal court, alleging retaliation for advocating voting rights; since we move the cases to federal court, the state court cannot go forward with its trial. The state court judge is unhappy that there is no trial, so he sentences me–without notice and in my absence–to ten days in jail and a $100 fine. A friend reads this in the local newspaper, and lets me know.

Early Monday morning, someone calls the office, asks whether I'm there, and hangs up. I suspect that Deputy Sheriff Bright has come to arrest me (and perhaps to place marijuana in my possession), so I head to the restaurant across the street, order breakfast and watch. Sure enough, Deputy Bright shows up. I stay away, and Armand goes to federal court and gets an order that they leave me alone. Then Armand gets a federal court to invalidate all the arrests, including the marijuana charges.

We tell this story in articles in a recent book, "Voices of Civil Rights Lawyers." Quite simply, this sheriff, this county prosecutor and this county judge create false charge after false charge, in an effort to suppress the African American community–and arrest its lawyers. Justice is distorted, justice is denied, justice is destroyed.

Armand and I continue to work for voting rights. After the Voting Rights Act, the City of Canton faces a municipal election with African Americans as a majority of registered voters, so the city expands its boundaries, bringing in almost 100 new white voters. Armand and I file suit, based on Sections 4 and 5 of the Voting Rights Act, prohibiting changes that are not reviewed and approved by the United States Department of Justice. We lose at trial, but Armand wins in the United States Supreme Court, in the first case applying the Act to municipal elections. Perkins v. Matthews, 400 U.S. 379 (1970).

Armand and I work together for several years. In the 1970s, LCDC closes and Armand and his wife Mary Frances move to her hometown, Charleston, South Carolina. Armand continues to work for civil rights, including further desegregation of Mississippi's colleges and universities, and for voting rights, including cases across the nation. Armand and I remain friends.

CHAPTER 9.

After four years with LCDC, I am offered the position as Executive Director of North Mississippi Rural Legal Services (NMRLS) in Oxford. In 1970, I move to Oxford, buy my first house, and find myself in charge of five offices with 40 employees: attorneys, community workers and support staff. Our mission is to apply the rule of law in an effort to reduce and eliminate the causes and consequences of poverty.

In Mississippi, the poorest state, legal assistance for poor people is controversial from the beginning. In 1966, Ole Miss Law School gets a new Dean, Josh Morse, who obtains War on Poverty money for Legal Aid and Ford Foundation money for five recent Yale Law School graduates to add to the faculty: Walter Dellinger (later Solicitor General of the United States), Joe Chubb (my college roommate), Mike Trister, George Strickler and Fred McLain. Mike and George lead the Legal Aid office and file school desegregation cases in Oxford and the surrounding county, attempting to improve educational opportunity. The white power structure does not like this, and complains to Ole Miss Chancellor Porter Fortune; the Chancellor orders Dean Morse to fire Mike and George and close down Legal Aid; Dean Morse follows this order, reluctantly; and Armand and I sue, on behalf of Mike and George. We lose at trial but win in the Court of Appeals, since law school teachers do a lot of outside work and it is discrimination to ban this one particular form of outside work. Trister v. University of Mississippi, 420 F.2d 499 (5th Cir. 1969). Armand then goes to the American Association of Law Schools, and the Association censures the law school.

Legal Aid separates from Ole Miss and becomes NMRLS, with continued federal funds and offices in Oxford, Holly Springs, Batesville, West Point and Greenwood. When NMRLS files 25 to 30 school desegregation cases across North Mississippi, Governor John Bell Williams responds with a 90-page complaint to the source of federal funds, the Office of Economic Opportunity (OEO). In 1970, just as I arrive at NMRLS, OEO investigates the Governor's complaint and produces a 270-page report that concludes that NMRLS is doing just what it is supposed to do.

Mike Trister leaves to work for the newly-established Children's Defense Fund in Washington, and I become Executive Director for NMRLS. As Mike is leaving, we file a challenge to Mississippi's plan to provide Medicaid coverage for children on public assistance but to exclude the single parent or caretaker who shares in and manages the assistance grant. This violates the federal government's requirement that Medicaid should include "all individuals whose needs are included in the subsistence grant." Triplett v. Cobb, 331 F.Supp. 652 (N.D.Ms.1971). We win this case, extending medical benefits to more than 20,000 parents and caretakers with needy children. Although public assistance remains limited, with a maximum of $50 per month for a family of four, the food benefits from the food stamp program and the medical benefits from Medicaid help to keep people alive.

Mike Trister hires John Brittain when he graduates from Howard University Law School, and John promptly becomes a brilliant lawyer who earns universal respect. Mike and I hire several other Howard Law School graduates, as well as several Ole Miss Law School graduates, African American and white. I hire David Lipman, a promising young graduate from Pennsylvania, but he faces a year-long waiting period before he can even take the bar exam; we sue and invalidate the waiting period, since it applies only to people from out of state. We become one of the very best programs in the country, winning many significant cases, struggling to bring the scales of justice into balance.

CHAPTER 10.

How do we eliminate the causes and effects of poverty? We focus on school desegregation, to expand educational opportunity.

Mississippi reluctantly begins "freedom-of-choice" desegregation in 1965, when I drive the African American students to the formerly white high school in McComb. By 1968, the United States Supreme Court recognizes that freedom-of-choice has limited effect, that only a few students desegregate, and that white children do not choose the schools formerly assigned to African Americans. In 1968, the Supreme Court decides that schools must eliminate all race-based boundaries and all race-based distinctions, if there is to be equal educational opportunity, consistent with Brown v. Board of Education, 347 U.S. 483 (1954)("separate educational facilities are inherently unequal").

For the 1970-1971 school year, federal courts require Mississippi school districts to prepare new plans for complete desegregation. Most districts decide to follow the standard school desegregation plan that is approved by the Court of

Appeals, and this resolves most of our school desegregation cases.

However, some districts resist the standard plan. For example, Carroll County adopts a plan that sends young men to one school and young women to another, and the African American community asks us to challenge this. At trial, our young attorney John McCreery asks the school superintendent why he separates students by gender, and the superintendent answers, "You know." John asks, "I don't know, please tell me why." Answer: "Don't you read the paper, don't you know about Detroit?" Question: "What about your county, Carroll County?" Answer: "People want this." Question: "Which people?" Answer: "White people." Question: "Why do they want this?" Answer: "You know." Question: "I don't know, please tell me." The superintendent turns to the federal judge and asks, "Do I really have to answer?" The judge says, "Yes, you do." The superintendent then turns to John and answers, "Because we don't want black boys sitting next to white girls." John turns toward me and asks what to do next. I say, "No further questions." The judge says that he doesn't want this desegregation plan to go to the Court of Appeals, and that the school district should just follow the standard plan.

This concern–"we don't want black boys sitting next to white girls"–is an obvious race-based stereotype, reflecting a white fear and smear. I later learn that President Eisenhower communicates this same white fear and smear to Supreme

Court Chief Justice Earl Warren, while the United States Supreme Court is considering Brown v. Board of Education. At dinner, President Eisenhower explains to the Chief Justice that white southerners "are not bad people. All they are concerned about is to see that their sweet little girls are not required to sit in school alongside some big overgrown Negro."

This white fear and smear arises in another school desegregation case, when the Coffeeville School District also proposes separate schools for male and female students. One day, our receptionist tells me that a man who shares my name, James Lewis, has come to see me. He is an African American teacher from Coffeeville, a community that is upset by this proposed plan and by the demotion of Mr. Lewis and other African American educators. So I meet with the community, file the school desegregation case, and take the superintendent's deposition. This superintendent testifies that he does not know why he chooses to separate males and females in the schools; he never reads an educational article about this; he talks to white people about it but cannot remember what they say; and he doesn't know about the Carroll County example. Despite all my questions, he gives no reason for his decision to separate the sexes.

When it's time for trial, 100 members of the African American community attend, filling every seat in the courtroom including the jury box, with an overflow waiting in our office across the street. I call community members, old and young, to testify why they object to this plan. Then I call a Harvard-trained sociologist, teaching at Vanderbilt University in Nashville, as an expert. He explains what sociologist Gunnar Myrdal sets out in "An American Dilemma," a classic study of race in America: the "rank order of discrimination." Myrdal describes racial discrimination as an attempt by the white community to protect itself from the following, ranked from extreme importance to general importance: (1) intermarriage or sex involving an African American man and a white woman; (2) social equality and respect for African Americans; (3) sharing public facilities, such as schools, churches and transportation; (4) sharing political opportunity; (5) equal treatment by law enforcement and the courts; and (6) equal economic opportunity, as to employment or property. Based on Myrdal's rank order, the expert concludes that the white community and its school leaders are practicing racial discrimination when they oppose having white and African American students together, particularly African American males and white females.

This is a thoughtful analysis of racism, and the judge and the audience listen attentively. The judge rules, as in Carroll County, that the district must follow the standard desegregation order and must reinstate the educators who have been demoted. Almost two decades later, the judge writes in his memoir that sex separation in Coffeeville is "vigorously objected to by blacks, who organized and maintained a school and merchant boycott [that] induced the court to eliminate assignment by sex!"

The white power structure considers interracial activity to be "race mixing," particularly if an African American male is involved. Many people, including Dollard, Myrdal, President Eisenhower and the Carroll County Superintendent, acknowledge that white people fear interracial activity. This fear of "mixing"–civil rights workers are often called "mixers"–motivates much of the white violence across the south, as well as the lynching of Mack Charles Parker and the too-swift injustice applied to Alfred Windom.

Despite white fear and white opposition, we succeed in desegregating many school districts, applying the standard plan and establishing the principle that districts must discontinue race-based distinctions. When a school district tries to have separate white and African American classrooms within its schools, we bring an end to this; when another school suspends every African American student who gets into a dispute with a white student, we bring an end to this. We win many battles, but many white students leave the public schools and move to private schools, "segregation academies."

I begin to see some beneficial effects from school desegregation. African American students learn that white students are advantaged but not inherently superior. African American law students at Ole Miss find that they are prepared to compete. White people may spread supremacist mythology, in order to support advantage and segregation, but these myths begin to fall away when confronted with reality. Teachers begin to see the actual strengths and weaknesses of each student, regardless of race. School desegregation helps many students. Research supports this conclusion.

CHAPTER 11.

Sometimes, educational opportunity is simply about education itself, rather than desegregation. In 1969, I teach a seminar on law and society at Tougaloo College, examining our Constitution within our society. I enjoy this course, and so do the students. One student, Bennie Thompson, goes on to become county supervisor, state legislator and United States Congressman, where he continues to serve with great distinction, including chairing the Select Commitee to Investigate the January 6 Attack on the United States Capitol.

In 1970, I offer to teach civil rights courses at Ole Miss Law School for free, while I'm at Legal Services. When Ole Miss rejects my offer, a friendly professor invites me to give guest lectures in constitutional law and to lead classes in a seminar on social welfare legislation. The law school dean cannot forbid guest lectures, but the dean does complain that I "don't know how to take no for an answer." And the dean is correct: I tend to challenge the answer "no," if it doesn't seem to be reasonable.

At Ole Miss, I find that most law students are open for discussion about the Constitution and about social welfare legislation. They are more thoughtful than the generation in power. I enjoy this teaching, and so do the students.

CHAPTER 12.

In 1964, Ole Miss professor James Silver writes a book that accurately describes Mississippi as a "closed society." The white power structure enforces segregation and supremacy at all costs, punishing any dissent by a white person or an African American. In fact, the state establishes a Sovereignty Commission to spy on and fight the civil rights movement. Years later, I get a copy of my Sovereignty Commission file, approximately 80 pages, when a federal court determines that the state's spying violates the First Amendment and that targets should have their individual files.

We struggle to open this closed society. We place faith in the First Amendment, protecting "the right of the people peaceably to assemble, and to petition their Government for a redress of grievances." Through peaceable assembly, such as our demonstrations in Magnolia and Jackson in 1965, people seek to expand the opportunity to vote, and the white power structure responds with arrests and suppression. When people protest in Leland, the power structure responds with tear gas. When people protest in Shelby, the power structure responds with an unlawful curfew. When fifty people protest in Holly Springs, the power structure responds with mass arrest and false charges. When several hundred students at Mississippi Valley State College protest peacefully, the power structure arrests them all and sends them to nearby Parchman Penitentiary, until Armand gets them released. When

75 people in Starkville protest peacefully, the power structure arrests them all, so we get the federal court to order prompt release for the people and to invalidate the arrests. When 50 people protest peacefully in Coffeeville and are arrested, at the time of the Coffeeville school desegregation case, I go to federal court that day to get these arrests set aside and to have the people released.

Yes, the power structure tries to maintain this closed society, unless the courts instruct them to respect the law. So LCDC, NMRLS and other civil rights lawyers remain busy representing peaceful protestors in community after community. These peaceful protestors would like food, information and prompt release, as I know from my times in jail, so I provide this each time I'm involved. I enjoy helping these protestors, as they try to wake up their community and push for a better way forward.

CHAPTER 13.

There is also protest within schools. At Delta State College in Cleveland, 50 African American students and one white student "sit in" at the president's office, protesting racial discrimination in the formerly all-white college. The school threatens expulsion, and this requires a "due process" hearing. The students ask me to represent them, but the school says that I'm not allowed to speak or ask questions. This is not a reasonable limitation, so I speak when I wish, and the school simply turns off the tape recorder when I speak. I also ask all the students to speak during the hearing, to voice their concerns about discrimination. Because we all speak, the school learns a lot about student life during desegregation, and the school comes to a reasonable decision: one week suspension.

White students also dissent within their schools. In Tupelo, three white high school student-leaders form a rock band and grow their hair long enough to touch the collar, despite a school rule. They are suspended and come to see me. I get a federal court order returning them to school, awaiting trial. At trial, an English teacher explains that she cannot maintain eye contact if a student's hair touches the collar, and I ask on cross-examination whether she can maintain eye contact with me–we can–even though my hair touches my collar. The chemistry teacher explains that hair touching the collar could catch on fire from a Bunsen burner, and I ask on cross-examination whether they allow girls to take chemistry–they do; I ask whether girls have hair touching the collar–they do; and I ask whether girls catch fire in chemistry–they don't. We appear to have reason on our side, but the Court of Appeals decides that long hair is an expressive right only in college, so we lose.

In Jackson, white students start an underground newspaper, "Kudzu." The city arrests them for printing "obscene" words and for vagrancy by distributing the paper. Armand and I file a class action to protect the right to write and dissent, the federal district court dismisses the case, and the Court of

Appeals reverses, saying this is a legitimate First Amendment claim. The newspaper is able to continue to print.

Older white people also dissent. Kent Saxon files a state court "taxpayer" case without a lawyer, challenging his county supervisors for using public property to do work for a few private citizens. The county court throws his case out without a trial, and the Mississippi Supreme Court reverses, saying that he does state a legitimate claim. Kent tries the case without a lawyer, loses, appeals, and asks LCDC to represent him on appeal. We submit our brief on appeal, and the Supreme Court reverses again. The county judge, rather frustrated, orders me to come for a contempt hearing, because our appeal criticizes his decision. Armand and I visit the Chief Justice of the Mississippi Supreme Court, who agrees that criticism during an appeal is a matter only for the court that considers the appeal, not the court that is criticized, and the Chief Justice lets us know that he will step in if we need help. Then Armand and I go to the county court contempt hearing; the judge asks me to read what we wrote in the appeal; I read it; the judge asks me to apologize, and I say, "If this is fair argument, as I intended, I don't need to apologize, but if it's too personal, I don't intend it to be and I apologize." The judge is not sure what to do with this conditional apology, so he asks me to repeat my apology, and I say the same thing. The judge drops the contempt charge. And decades later, the federal government convicts a number of county supervisors for similar conduct, the use of public property to benefit a few private citizens. Kent Saxon: you are right.

What about freedom of speech at public colleges? Mississippi requires every speaker to have the approval of the school administration. The national office of the American Civil Liberties Union (ACLU) challenges this, and the federal court strikes down this limit. Student groups then invite me to speak at several colleges, and I particularly remember the University of Southern Mississippi in Hattiesburg, where I am the first unapproved speaker in school history. I sit at the edge of the auditorium stage with a microphone and say to 300 people, "What would you like to talk about?" For several hours, people present questions, ideas and concerns, and we have an exhilarating public discussion, honoring freedom of thought, coming away better for it.

What about the ACLU itself? We establish a State Chapter, and I serve on the Board and as General Counsel. For the ACLU, I write and distribute "Your Student Rights" on a regular basis, discussing developments in the law about due process, freedom of thought and freedom of expression. We are trying to open up this "closed society," to create room for differing thoughts and opinions.

Years later, I find that the Sovereignty Commission obtains the minutes of ACLU meetings. Yes, the closed society spies on the ACLU, in an effort to remain closed.

CHAPTER 14.

We also try to ensure decent treatment in prison. I visit Parchman Penitentiary several times to see clients. And in late 1971, I step down from NMRLS and explore what to do next. Roy Haber of the Lawyers Committee for Civil Rights Under Law asks me to come to Jackson and help organize a big case challenging prison conditions at Parchman, to pull together the facts and the law. We tour the penitentiary with an expert, Robert Sarver, who worked toward reform in Arkansas prisons. We find that Parchman is completely segregated, despite a United States Supreme Court decision in 1968 that requires jail and prison desegregation, and despite federal law, Title VI of the Civil Rights Act of 1964, that forbids federal funding to segregated recipients; due to this segregation, the Mississippi Department of Corrections could lose all its federal funds. We also find that the prison is a big cotton plantation, using inmate labor, making a profit for the state. We see inmates loading onto flatbed trucks, heading to work in the cotton fields, where inmates with guns–called "trusties"–will ensure that they work hard picking cotton. And the inmates all live in large dormitories, with 20 double-decker beds per room, and with no protection from each other. Food and sanitation are deplorable.

After I help Roy Haber organize the facts and law, he proceeds with the case, leading to substantial reform. Gates v. Collier, 501 F.2d 1291 (5thCir.1974). The Court of Appeals, quoting independent experts, describes conditions at Parchman as "philosophically, psychologically, physically, racially and morally intolerable." The court requires significant reform, but this prison remains a particularly horrible place, compared to other prisons in this country.

I return to Oxford. We establish the Mississippi Prison Project, receiving many letters from inmates at Parchman. We interview inmates to see whether we can help. One inmate seems quite young. When I ask, he says that he has been at Parchman since age 16 for burglary. I ask why he isn't considered a juvenile and sent to a juvenile institution, and he says that no one ever asks his age. I file a petition in state court, since he should have been considered as a juvenile. The state judge calls me and asks for his birth certificate; when I send this, the state judge orders his immediate release. Yes, I'm haunted by the fact that no one asks his age, not the judge, not a prosecutor, not a defense attorney, not a family representative, and not the penitentiary when they receive him.

CHAPTER 15.

I serve a purpose in Mississippi, working toward economic, political, educational and social opportunity for all people. Can I leave? In mid-1973, my life changes. At my cousin Harold's wedding in New York, I meet his neighbor, Connie Milstein. We elope back to Oxford with her young daughter Abigail, and we marry under a tree on the Ole Miss campus.

Where should we live? We decide to travel around the Southeast, looking for the best place for our family. We consider opportunities in Macon and Atlanta, Georgia, Knoxville, Tennessee, Columbia, South Carolina and Durham, North Carolina, and we decide that Durham offers something positive for each of us. In January 1974, we move. I go to work for a Mississippi friend who now runs Durham Legal Aid; Connie applies to and enrols in North Carolina Central University School of Law; Abigail starts at pre-school; and I am soon offered a fellowship at Duke University School of Law.

As I leave Mississippi, I know that it is changing, getting somewhat better. In 1964, President Johnson directs the FBI to infiltrate the Klan and solve civil rights crimes, and the United States Department of Justice successfully prosecutes the Deputy Sheriff and Klansmen responsible for the 1964 murders of James Chaney, Michael Schwerner and Andrew Goodman. There are a few federal prosecutions for similar civil rights crimes, holding Klansmen accountable for racial violence. Violence decreases. Furthermore, segregation is no longer the absolute principle. Schools are desegregated, more than schools in much of the country. Public places are desegregated by law, Title II of the Civil Rights Act of 1964. The legal community is desegregated, since Ole Miss, Howard and other schools begin to produce more African American lawyers. The political process is desegregated, since the African American community responds to the Voting Rights Act with massive registration. In the 1967 election and subsequent elections, there are many successful African

American candidates, and the African American community gains genuine political power and voice.

I have served some–only some–of the purpose that brought me to Mississippi in 1965. I move on.

CHAPTER 16.

I'd like to jump forward in time, and say more about Mississippi. In 1992, 1994, 1998, 2005, 2009, 2012 and 2014, I return to Mississippi with Arden and our family. Yes, dear reader, my marriage to Connie will fail after five years, and two years after this failure, Arden will come back into my life. We will marry and form a family: Heather Esme, David and Kate. Details will follow in due course.

In 1992, Arden, David, Kate and I drive through Mississippi on our way back from Florida to Illinois, and we visit with Ms. Quin in McComb and with a Delta Ministry friend, Rims Barber, in Jackson. In 1994, we attend a 30-year reunion in Jackson for LCDC staff and volunteers, and have lunch with Harry Bowie. In 1998, Arden and I drive through Oxford on our way to Florida, and we spend one day watching our daughter Heather Esme, a young public interest lawyer, trying a case together with the National Prison Project, successfully challenging conditions on death row at Parchman Penitentiary.

In 2005, Arden and I go to a Mississippi Center for Justice Dinner that is also the 40-year reunion for the Lawyers Committee for Civil Rights Under Law. While there, about 40 of us visit the Chief Judge of the local federal court, Henry Wingate, an African American from Jackson and Yale Law School, and he talks with us for almost two hours about civil rights issues in the community. We discuss the controversial mural that has been in the federal courtroom for 70 years, depicting a plantation owner and family in the middle, white artisans to the left, and African Americans picking cotton on the right; this mural depicts enslavement, serfdom and segregation, and is extremely offensive. Chief Judge Wingate keeps it undraped because he wants people to see the truth about the past. The next day, Guyot, Armand, Arden and I drive down to Brookhaven for dinner with Harry Bowie, who has severe diabetes, has lost a leg, and has a few months to live. Talking with Guyot, Armand and Harry helps to set me on track for a major speech that I am to give in Illinois on Martin Luther King's Birthday in 2006.

In spring 2009, Armand and I, along with Chokwe Lumumba, an African American lawyer and future Mayor of Jackson, speak to the Veterans of the Civil Rights Movement in Jackson, discussing the potential for justice in the Obama presidency. I say that we should expect "respect for the law, with openness about what is going on, and with proper checks and balances. But that's not enough–not enough. We should not simply and blindly enforce the law; we should also look at the impact of enforcing the law; look at the community impact of the law; look at the rates of incarceration, in this country and in the African American community and among young African Americans, and look at the assistance that we should provide to prisoners and families when these prisoners return to their communities, when they re-enter their communities; and we should demand that we as a people find a better way forward, with law enforcement that actually serves our communities....Let us raise our expectations, and let us push to see that the Department of Justice meets those expectations. People came together once before and reshaped Justice in Mississippi, so we know that people can come together once again and reshape Justice throughout this country." Dear reader, you will discover that I will become the United States Attorney in central Illinois from 2010 through 2016, and you will get to decide whether I meet these expectations.

In 2012, Arden, Kate and I drive south to Jackson, for a dinner and tour organized by the Mississippi Center for Justice. On our way, we stop at the National Civil Rights Museum in Memphis, telling the story of the struggle and ending at the Lorraine Motel where Dr. King was assassinated. As Arden, Kate and I drive from Memphis to Jackson, I point out town after town and describe struggle after struggle, feeling the enormous damage caused by centuries of white power and white supremacy. I am again haunted by the difficulty of daily life under these conditions, as well as the difficulty incurred during the struggle. My feelings remain deep and strong, and the lessons from Mississippi remain powerful within my mind, heart and soul.

At the Center for Justice dinner, I see an old friend, an African American lawyer who has recently become a federal district judge, and I've recently become a United States Attorney. I hug my friend, then I step back and say, "I've never hugged a federal judge before." His response: "I've never hugged a United States Attorney before."

In 2012, this Center for Justice tour ends in Oxford, just before the 50th anniversary of Meredith's 1962 desegregation of Ole Miss. The school has changed. There is a statue of Meredith in the middle of the campus, and a celebration of desegregation. White and African American students mingle. Yes, issues continue to arise. When football crowds wave confederate flags, the Chancellor decides that there should be no sticks in the football stadium, and this reduces the flag-waving. When there is concern about school monuments that honor an all-white past, a campus committee reaches a compromise that leaves the monuments in place but provides a plaque with full historical interpretation. Ole Miss is trying to face its struggles, its past, its present, and its future.

In 2014, Arden and I go to a 50th reunion for the workers and volunteers from Freedom Summer in 1964. Three hundred people gather for several days at Tougaloo College, for extraordinary discussions of where we were and where we are, connecting the past and the present. David Barnum attends with his wife Pushpika; David works in Holmes County in 1964 and southwest Mississippi in 1965, then lives at the

LCDC house and teaches political science at Tougaloo for several years. Armand Derfner attends with his son. And Brenda Travis, a friend from McComb, attends. A few years later, Brenda will publish her powerful memoir, "Mississippi's Exiled Daughter: How My Civil Rights Baptism Under Fire Shaped My Life," telling the story of her work alongside SNCC in McComb in 1961: how the white power structure gave her a choice of imprisonment or exile, and how she made a life for herself and her family after this "civil rights baptism under fire."

On the first day of this reunion, Bob Moses speaks. Bob leads SNCC's first effort in Mississippi, in McComb in 1961, and he leads SNCC's Freedom Summer in 1964. In 2014, Bob says that we are now in a "third constitutional age;" in the first constitutional age (1619-1865), this country accepts slavery; in the second constitutional age (1877-1961), this country accepts segregation and serfdom; and this third constitutional age begins with the civil rights movement and will continue as long as this country tries to live up to the promises in the thirteenth, fourteenth and fifteenth amendments to the United States Constitution. Then Bob leads us all in reciting the Preamble to the Constitution: "We the People of the United States, in Order to form a more perfect Union, establish Justice, insure domestic Tranquility, provide for the common defense, promote the general Welfare, and secure the Blessings of Liberty to ourselves and our Posterity, do ordain and establish this Constitution for the United States of America."

Bob focuses on the American promise, so long withheld, so long unfulfilled–and still to be pursued. Bob believes in the American promise. So do I. Bob recognizes and experiences the American tragedy–enslavement, exclusion, exploitation and injustice–that exists, despite the American promise. So do I.

On Thursday night, Arden, Armand, David, Pushpika and I visit an exhibition of Matt Herron's powerful photographs of the civil rights movement. We are on our way to the initial screening of "Dirt and Deeds in Mississippi," a documentary by David Schulman about African American landowners who support the civil rights movement in Holmes County. This documentary includes interviews with Armand, Guyot, Robert Clark, David Barnum and others, including me. At this movie, we reunite with Robert Clark and many others.

CHAPTER 17.

On Friday, Brenda Travis sees Anthony Quin, who attends because Matt Herron's most famous photograph shows Anthony's arrest in 1965 with the American flag at the Governor's Mansion; I include this photograph in the Photo section of this memoir. Brenda tells Anthony that I'm in town; Anthony calls me, we meet, and we have an incredibly intense ten-minute hug, trying to make up for decades of separation. We have dinner and catch up. I feel close to Anthony–again. He now uses his first name, Wayne, is married to Dianna, has twin children, Brianna and Wayne Junior, lives in Tampa, has a Ph.D., and is an educator. Ms. Quin has passed away.

For Sunday, Brenda arranges a civil rights commemoration in McComb at Society Hill Missionary Baptist Church, scene of a Klan bombing in 1964. I meet the former Mayor of McComb, an African American; the present Mayor, a white man; several students who desegregated the schools in 1965; Roy Lee's son; and many others. McComb has changed. Many people speak, and I get to speak after Wayne.

Wayne sends me a YouTube of a television interview that he does before he goes to the 2014 reunion. In this interview, he says that we became brothers in the 1960s. He's correct. Ms. Quin is a formative and formidable person in my life, and that makes us brothers.

In January 2015, I visit Wayne in Tampa and meet his older brother Cleotis Worthy. Cleotis lives his early years with his grandparents, sharecropping on rented property in Walthall County, growing cotton. The white landowner keeps all the financial records and allows the grandparents only to break even, despite excellent crops, so the family leaves and moves to McComb.

When I visit, Wayne is not well. He has been diagnosed with pancreatic cancer, and is fighting hard for his family. Church members come by and we all have a good day, but I am concerned as I leave. I keep in touch, but he passes away a few months later.

I miss him. I am proud to be his brother.

In January 2016, Arden and I visit Dianna, Brianna and Wayne Junior. We try every water ride at Tampa's Busch Gardens, and have a lot of fun. Although we are separated by many miles, I want to remain a good brother-in-law and uncle to Wayne's wonderful family.

Yes, I leave Mississippi, but I will carry the people and the lessons within me for the rest of my life.

CHAPTER 18.

I'd like to reflect.

The civil rights movement helps to establish genuine African American voice and genuine African American power. But the struggle continues. Public schools desegregate, but many white students choose private "segregation academies," diminishing support for public education. The vote is desegregated, so that Mississippi now has more African American elected officials than any other state, but the predominantly white Republican Party slowly builds a veto-proof majority in the state legislature. Like many other states across the nation, Mississippi is actively involved in efforts to suppress the vote, as well as efforts to invoke "whiteness" as the basis for a political cause. African Americans gain more opportunity, but the white power structure finds new ways to limit this opportunity.

Why does the change that accompanies the civil rights movement–a change that is widely applauded as bringing our reality closer to our ideals, bringing "what is" closer to "what should be"–now meet such resistance, even before the change is complete? For a partial answer, I return to John Dollard's "Caste and Class in a Southern Town," describing white economic, political, educational and social advantage. This advantage forms the basis for continuing resistance to full and equal economic, political, educational and social opportunity for all.

For me, the civil rights movement includes many of my "life teachers." Harry Bowie and Lawrence Guyot show me how to work with others toward social change, and Ms. Quin shows me how to lead a family and serve a community at the same time. Al Bronstein and Armand Derfner show me how to connect with people in trouble, to address and remedy injustice, and to serve justice. I am grateful to everyone I mention and everyone I remember but don't mention. They all help me, as I try to become the useful person that I wish to become.

Cain asks Adam and Eve, "Am I my brother's keeper?" In Mississippi, I learn my answer: we must work to make the world a better place for all our brothers, all our sisters, all our children, if we wish to be a decent member within the human family. This work matters.

4

NORTH CAROLINA (1974-1977) AND WASHINGTON (1977-1983)

CHAPTER 1.

In January 1974, Connie, Abigail and I settle into a nice new house in Durham. We like this part of North Carolina. It's educated and progressive. I work with good peaple at Legal Aid, and Connie applies to law schools in the area.

I take Abigail to and from pre-school, and we spend time together in the middle of our day, talking a lot. Abigail is bright and inquisitive, challenging my parenting skills. One day, a tooth comes loose, and we put it under her pillow. While she sleeps, I take the tooth and replace it with money. When she comes into our room the next day, she discovers that I have the tooth, and asks why. I make up an explanation, that I'm helping the tooth fairy.

A few weeks later, Abigail asks me about God. I say that many believe, but some do not. She asks more questions, and I acknowledge that I do not believe. A few weeks later, Abigail and Connie discuss God, Abigail repeats our discussion, and Connie is less than pleased.

CHAPTER 2.

After a few months, Duke's School of Law calls and offers a two-year teaching fellowship and a Master's degree, and I accept. At Duke, I begin by co-organizing and co-chairing a two-day Law and Aging conference, examining federal and state programs that serve the older population. This conference is sponsored by the law school, the Governor's Coordinating Council on Aging and Duke's Center for the Study of Aging and Human Development. We bring in experts on income maintenance, health care and a wide range of programs and services for our rapidly-increasing older population, and I edit the 100-page report describing this conference.

This conference looks at Social Security, an income replacement program that is based on work history, as well as the four "safety net" income assistance programs, created during the Great Depression for people in serious financial need who cannot or do not work, if the people fit into a specific category: (1) old (age 65) or (2) blind or (3) disabled or (4) families with only one parent or caretaker. Since the Depression, the states have operated these four categorical assistance programs and determined the benefit amounts, with generous federal financial support. But in the early 1970s, Congress takes the first three safety net programs, for the old or blind or disabled, and fully federalizes these, calling this Supplemental Security Income (SSI). This is a big improvement. In southern states with a history of limited benefits, SSI increases the benefit amounts, increases the number of people who meet the higher federal standard of financial need, and greatly increases the federal financial contribution. In North Carolina, for example, SSI increases the individual benefit by 50%, and the state jumps from about 30,000 elderly recipients to about 75,000 elderly SSI recipients.

But this improvement is incomplete. The fourth "safety net" program, Aid to Families with Dependent Children (AFDC)–I testified about this program before the Mississippi Chapter of the Commission on Civil Rights–does not improve. In 1970 and 1971, Congress considers federalizing and enriching AFDC–like SSI–through a "Family Assistance Program;" this passes the House of Representatives twice but fails in the Senate; as a consequence, needy families and needy children remain in the old state-federal program, with benefits limited by each state. For example, North Carolina calculates–this calculation is required by federal law–that a family with a parent and three children actually needs $625 per month for minimum subsistence, but the state limits the benefit to $284 for such families.

For many needy families and needy children, this gap between actual need and actual benefits will get significantly worse over time. In the 1980s, the President of the United States makes welfare a political issue, and in the 1990s, another President vows to "end welfare as we know it." As a consequence, the United States brings an end to AFDC, the fourth safety net program, and replaces it with temporary assistance, in the form of a block grant to each state. From these block grants, a limited amount of money actually reaches poor families.

Let's be clear: we know what is needed for families with dependent and vulnerable children, and we provide only a small fraction of what is needed. When we make this choice, the children must face the consequences. Why do we make this choice, despite our commitment to the "general welfare" in the Preamble to our Constitution? Because, in the real world, we are engaged in a struggle: the advantaged versus the disadvantaged.

CHAPTER 3.

At Duke, I teach a seminar in Law and Aging in 1975 and a seminar in Law and Poverty in 1976. I mix training in interviewing, counseling, negotiation and advocacy with substantive legal issues arising from aging and poverty. Students apply their education in the real world, assisting clients from the Center for the Study of Aging or from Legal Aid. I enjoy this teaching, because I believe that education needs to connect to the real world.

In the Law and Aging seminar, we read "On Death and Dying" by Elizabeth Kubler-Ross, and we discuss how people work through tragedy, loss and grief: denial, anger, bargaining, depression and finally acceptance. When I face significant difficulty in my life, I try to remember this process, face the difficulty, and move toward acceptance and the steps that need to follow.

Then, after two years at Duke–teaching seminars, taking courses, writing a Masters' thesis on law and poverty, and earning an LLM degree–I teach one year at North Carolina Central University School of Law, also in Durham. I teach civil procedure to first year students and trial practice and law and poverty to third year students, and I initiate the clinical program. This law school was originally for African Americans, in the era when a few southern states had "separate but equal" graduate schools. By the 1970s, the law schools are all integrated, particularly this law school, with approximately equal numbers of white and African American students. I enjoy teaching, because most students are training for general practice in their communities, serving real people in the real world. These students are highly motivated, and our classes are filled with good discussions.

In trial practice, I give an hour lecture and lead two hours of simulated practice each week, with students interviewing, preparing and questioning witnesses, choosing juries and making arguments. For the final exam, students try a simulated case that is designed for trial lawyers. I videotape this simulated trial and review it with the students, so that they will see themselves practicing law before they head into actual courtrooms. I believe that legal education should include this form of preparation, and I improve my own skills whenever I prepare a lecture, lead a discussion or review a videotape.

Connie takes this course, so I'm her teacher–and her spouse. This is okay, as long as I'm tactful with comments about her work. Connie is a good student, on law review, and earns a top grade.

Can we stay in North Carolina? Not really. Connie wants to explore other possibilities. I enjoy teaching but want to get back into courtrooms. So we look around again. After interviews for teaching and practice in many locations, we decide on Washington, D.C.

CHAPTER 4.

In November 1977, I go to work in the Civil Division of this country's largest law firm, the United States Department of Justice. In the first week, I read a law school textbook on my primary assignment, maritime law, and in the second week, my supervisor, Larry Ledebur, hands me twenty case files, asks me to prepare and try these cases, to come to him with any question, and to pick up more cases when I finish these.

These cases are large and challenging, spread across the country from Boston to Florida to Louisiana to Chicago. We protect rivers from oil spills and locks and dams from property damage. And we defend the United States, when people complain about the government. The facts and law are complex, but the basic issue is always responsibility, private or public, for damage.

I enjoy this work. I have the most cases in the section and travel regularly. I'm busy, perhaps too busy.

CHAPTER 5.

In 1978, Connie and I acknowledge that we are not growing together. I'm fine, Connie is fine, Abigail is fine, but we are not coming together with a common purpose. After a few discussions, we separate. I move to a nearby apartment, I continue to see Abigail often, and we formalize a simple divorce.

We begin with good intentions, but fail at marriage. This is difficult and painful. Why do I fail? I want–I need–to understand. I talk with my brother Steve and his wife Jane, who suggest consulting a psychiatrist. I do, and the psychiatrist suggests group therapy, for an hour, three days a week.

Who am I? I understand facts and law, but do I understand myself? I can start with some objective facts, then how I feel about these facts and how group therapy affects me.

Dad's father, Grandpa Nathan, comes from Russia–an area that is now part of Ukraine–to New York when still young, and his family changes their name from Levinsky to Lewis. Grandpa goes to work in silk processing, is succeful, and marries Grandma May. They ensure that their three children, Stephen, Arthur and Jean, get a good education.

Mom's father, Grandpa Jack, and her mother, Grandma Rosalie, come from families that settled in this country generations ago. Grandpa grows up in Johnstown, Pennsylvania, where his father has a dry goods store. In 1889, the Johnstown flood sweeps away their home and store; they climb on the roof of their home, float downriver, survive and rebuild. A few years later, the family moves to New York; Grandpa studies law at Columbia; he meets and marries Grandma, and they also ensure that their three children, Jay, Desna and Dan, get a good education. We are close with Mom's family.

Mom and Dad, Stephen and Desna, are both born in Brooklyn. They meet as teenagers. Mom is bright and beautiful, with strong social skills. Dad is brilliant, and starts college (Princeton) at age 16. Mom and Dad begin to date while Dad is in college, and they marry when Mom is 19 and Dad is 22. Mom discontinues her education and maintains their home, while Dad works with his father in silk processing. They are comfortable, even through the Great Depression. My brother Steve is born in 1936, and I'm born in 1940.

During World War II, Dad enlists in the Navy. Because he has business experience, the Navy asks him to order equipment and material, so he serves in upstate New York and then in Pennsylvania, and we are able to move with him and stay together during the war. After the war, Dad starts a hosiery business, then a knitwear business, and does very well. We move to a New York suburb, New Rochelle, and then to another suburb, Scarsdale.

When I'm in high school and Steve is in college (Princeton), Dad asks whether we'd like to learn and take over the knitwear business. We decline, gently. A few years later, Dad sells the business and remains as a consultant, but the new owners do not do well, so Dad buys the business back, builds it up again, sells it and retires.

These are objective facts. What's behind these facts? Why would I be uncomfortable with being comfortable?

When I'm young, Mom and Dad delegate much of the parenting to Elizabeth and George, an African American couple from North Carolina who live with us and take care of our household. They get us started in the morning, drive us where we need to go, clean the house and prepare and serve the meals. When I'm little, Elizabeth supervises my bath. When I run away from school in first grade, Elizabeth meets me at home and applies a hairbrush to my bottom. When I climb a rope into a tree, Elizabeth puts a snack in a paper bag and I pull it up my rope. When Elizabeth wants to go fishing, we go together to a nearby lake. In the morning, Elizabeth looks at my eyes, to see whether they are gray, green or blue, and tells me my mood for the day, sad, mischievous or sunny. Then she asks me what I'd like for breakfast.

Yes, I attach to my parents, my brother Steve and my dog Rusty, but I also attach to Elizabeth and George. At age 8, I'm quite surprised when Mom fires them. I'm shocked that you could fire members of the family.

Mom and I don't discuss the firing. As I grow up, I hear that Elizabeth and George get ready too early, preparing for a Sunday afternoon off, but I don't think this is the real reason for firing them. Instead, I think that Mom realizes that she isn't doing enough to raise her two sons, and fires Elizabeth and George in an attempt to regain authority. It doesn't work. Steve is already on his independent path, and I'm just confused.

I soon run away again. For several hours, I walk around town with a small suitcase. When it gets dark, I call Mom and she comes and gets me. Instead of a hairbrush or other discipline, Mom starts me with a child psychologist. He asks me to draw a picture of my family, and I put Mom, Dad and Steve on one side and myself on the other. I know that the psychologist is supposed to advise Mom on parenting, but it's probably a bit late, since my independent streak is already established.

Mom maintains friendly contact with Elizabeth. Years later, I come up from Mississippi, and Mom invites Elizabeth for lunch. We have a good visit. Many years later, Mom reads "The Help," a story about white employers and African American household employees in Mississippi, and Mom says to me that she may have been mistaken in firing Elizabeth and George. I agree, and we move on to another subject.

I love Mom. When she dies in 2016 at age 103, I speak at Ferncliff, where Dad is also interred, saying that she was lovable and occasionally a bit annoying. Many in the family remain close to her throughout her life. I would still like to be able to call her on a Sunday, and see how she's doing.

I love Dad. He's a complex person, often unknowable. He is troubled and drinks too much. I go to work with him one summer when I am 16, and I'm astonished when he orders two double martinis at lunch and then has more to drink when he gets home. As I get older, I begin to understand his drinking as sedation to help him live with some mysterious trouble.

I have glimpses, but only glimpses, of a father who is sweet and loving. In 1996, I speak at his funeral, with much love: "I remember a thin, handsome man in a Navy uniform; he was very tall, or I was very small; he was my father....I remember giving Dad a kiss every night, when he came home from work, and I remember going to the train station to pick him up, when I could drive....I remember driving home from college and informing Mom and Dad that I was going to quit, and I remember Dad informing me that I wasn't, and I remember following Dad's suggestion that I get back in the car and finish what I'd started....I remember learning that I wasn't going to get a long explanation from my Father, but if I provoked him properly when I was young or understood him properly when I grew up, I would find out what he was thinking and what he was feeling; and I certainly remember that under his surface was a very sweet and very loving and very caring and very gentle person....And I want his grandchildren to know that he delighted, with a quiet but very deep delight, in your exploits and in your very existence....Dad loved you all very deeply and found you all to be a real source of joy....I remember Katie's bat mitzvah this June; Dad had said an Aliyah for Jonnie and Robbie and Jennifer, and he wanted to say an Aliyah for Katie; at the bat mitzvah, I spoke about the gift of life, that had been passed down to us from our ancestors in Africa and the Middle East and Russia and Europe; I say today that Dad had that gift of life, and he accepted that gift and experienced all its joys and all its sorrows; Mom and Dad passed that gift on to Steve and myself and through Jane and Arden on to his grandchildren and great-grandchildren and on to a future that we cannot see and do not know; and Dad treated this gift of life with great respect, and understood that we must love one another and care for one another and help one another."

I have love in my past, and some loss as well.

Steve sets his own course. While in medical school, he meets Jane, and they are delighted with each other. They marry when he is 24 and she is 20, and they build a strong marriage and wonderful family with three children, Jon, Robert and Jennifer. Steve and Jane are now retired, and they have six grandchildren and two great-granchildren. I call them each Sunday, just as I called Mom and Dad.

Who am I, and what do I believe? When young, I formulate a simple bedtime prayer: "God bless Mommy and Daddy and Steve and our dog Rusty and everyone who does the world good." As I grow, I have questions. When I read John Hersey's description of the Holocaust and the Atomic Bomb, I have questions. When my college freshman philosophy course introduces me to the concept of free will, I have questions. When I study Greek thought, I have questions. I may hope and pray for good, but who will do this good?

In Mississippi, I begin to form my answer, as you see in this memoir: we must come together alongside others and work toward the common good. In Judaism–we are Jewish–this is Tikkun Olam, the obligation to repair the world. Judaism teaches that we may not complete this work in our lifetime, but we may not desist from the effort.

This still leaves questions about myself. Group therapy is a safe place to explore questions, issues and feelings, and perhaps to repair myself. I don't have any particular breakthrough, but I slowly become more comfortable with my past, gentler with my feelings, and more assured that I can connect my feelings with my reality. This is a slow and steady process, and takes five years.

In group therapy, we try to examine our dreams. This interests me, since I read Sigmund Freud's "The Interpretation of Dreams" while in high school, learning that dreams are revealing.

I do recall a few recent dreams: I'm in school, usually Harvard, and it's time for final exams, but I haven't gone to class or read the material, and I don't even know when and where the exam will be. This is a not-uncommon anxiety dream, about being unprepared for a test or obligation. In a similar dream, I work on a British ship but I don't do my chores, so they tell Queen Elizabeth II–is she Elizabeth from my childhood–and she comes to remind me to do my work. These dreams connect to my experience, coming home with 99s on seventh grade final exams, and Dad asking only, "What did you get wrong?" From dreams and experience, I know that I must do my work and get it 100% right.

I have another set of disturbing dreams, that I cannot find love.

CHAPTER 6.

I can find love. Or love can find me.

Arden! In February 1980, I get a letter–the all-time best letter. She's in law school, looking for a summer job in Washington. Do I have any suggestions? I call immediately, and we begin frequent and lengthy telephone calls. We're both divorced. In March, she comes to Washington to spend spring break with her brother Gordon, and we have long walks and long talks. I know that I'm falling in love, and I tell her. She feels this, and we cherish our feelings. This time, this second chance, I'm determined to be the best possible boyfriend.

After spring break, Arden returns to Illinois and law school. We talk frequently, and I come out to visit. I meet Arden's children, Heather Esme and David, ages 7 and 5. They're cute, funny, challenging and wonderful. I visit again and again, and we begin to think ahead. We become engaged. At some point, Arden lets on that before she writes, she does a search to be sure that I'm single. My response: "Thank you for finding me."

In May 1981, we have a simple wedding in Arden's home, with family and some good friends. And we have a wonderful honeymoon. We borrow Steve and Jane's sailboat and explore Long Island Sound. One day, we sail slowly up the Connecticut River, heading for a quiet cove. As we approach the cove, several swans swim alongside. Then we spend a few days in New York City, followed by a few days with Heather Esme and David in the Wisconsin Dells.

I continue to work from Washington and spend weekends and vacations in Illinois. I have an enormous case in the midwest, arising from an extraordinary blizzard and ice blockage in the Ohio River, and I also have a series of cases from a lock and dam in the Ohio River, so I see Arden on a weekend, work in Cincinnati or Louisville for a week, and then return to Arden each weekend. This sustains us while Arden finishes law school, and I look for jobs in Illinois so that we could have a home together.

Then we become pregnant! On Thursday, April 21, 1983, I fly to Chicago from depositions in Louisiana, knowing that Katie's birth is imminent. At 4:30 the next morning, Arden wakes and starts to get ready to go to the hospital in Chicago, later in the day. At 7:30, Heather asks Arden just the right question: "Are you having a contraction?" "Yes, and it's strong." We immediately jump in the car, drop Heather and David with a good friend, and speed from the suburb toward the hospital. But we can't make it to Chicago, so we pull into the Evanston Hospital. I run into the Emergency Room and say that my wife is giving birth in the car (not quite true). Within five minutes, Arden is delivering Katie in the Emergency Room. It's Earth Day, April 22, 1983.

I spend the next month with Arden, Heather Esme, David and Katie. And my job search succeeds. The United States

Attorney in Springfield, Gerry Fines, is looking for a civil attorney, and he chooses me. On August 15, 1983, I move from Washington to Springfield.

5

SPRINGFIELD (1983-2010)

CHAPTER 1.

I spend the first night alone in our empty house, sleeping on the floor. The next morning, Arden arrives from Chicago with her mother Millie as well as Heather, David and Katie, followed by a moving van, and we quickly fill up the house. Across the street, Heather and David find six girls along with two little boys. Next door, David finds a boy his age. And we find a nearby Chuck-E-Cheese, plus some local restaurants with flaming desserts. We begin to settle in.

Arden's best friend from Chicago, Bobbie Schachter, has a cousin in Springfield, Fred Benson. Fred and his wife Terri introduce us to lots of nice people with lots of nice children. We find everything we need, and Springfield becomes our home. I consider these the best years of my life and our lives, particularly when we come together around the kitchen table for dinner, talking about our day.

CHAPTER 2.

Work is quite interesting. I bring along several large cases from Washington, in order to finish these. The United States Attorney's Office also has challenging cases. Gerry Fines, the United States Attorney, is knowledgeable and friendly, and my new colleagues are talented and helpful. It's an excellent office.

I get ready for trial in my largest case from Washington, arising from the extraordinary blizzard and ice blockage in the Ohio River, causing damage along 80 miles of river. Early in the case, 100 lawyers pursue claims against the government. When it's time for trial, I write and send 300 pages of trial brief to the court, then I pack up fifteen boxes of evidence, drive to Cincinnati, try the case against six of the lawyers for a full week, and return, doing this five times spread over six months. At the end, the judge decides against the government, awarding approximately $2 million, but the Court of Appeals reverses and decides for the government, agreeing with the first issue that I raise, "discretionary function," protecting the very difficult decisions that the Corps of Engineers has to make during this extraordinary blizzard and this unprecedented ice blockage.

I have a good time at work, amid good people. After a few months, Gerry Fines comes and asks me whether I'd like to be the District's first Civil Chief. I'm not looking to be a Chief. Gerry offers me a free parking space next to the building, and this persuades me to say yes.

This begins a twenty-five year career as Civil Chief. I take most of the "ugly and expensive" cases. When the government is right, we say so and go to trial. When the government is wrong, we say so and settle. We try to provide answers that are prompt, fact-based, supported by reason, clear and fair. This is good government, and should please those who believe in justice–and surprise those who are cynical.

CHAPTER 3.

Arden gets us all organized, with Heather and David in school and Katie growing quickly. After several months, a friend tells Arden that there is part-time work at the State Appellate Defender's Office. Arden interviews and is hired, beginning a thirty-year career arguing criminal appeals for indigent defendants, making sure that the law is followed and that justice is done. She corrects many injustices, such as the lengthy sentence given Lee Otis Griffin when his lawyer decides to misrepresent Lee in an attempt to protect another defendant. Arden gains his freedom–and his friendship.

Heather makes friends at her new school, and finds that she is one of the best students. She also plays an excellent tombstone–"please don't take me for granite"–in the sixth-grade play. When I tell Heather stories about my mischief during school, she responds that she takes school seriously and doesn't really appreciate my stories; I learn to keep stories about mischief to myself. Another time, I chastise Heather for a bit of misconduct, and she responds that she gets the point and I should shorten the lecture. Yes, I learn to listen to her, as I try to become a better parent.

David hangs out at the tether-ball court at his new school, making new friends. With these friends, he moves on to skateboarding, garage-band music, juggling and the unicycle. In his sixth-grade play, he is the rear end of a horse and entertains the audience at intermission with his juggling. He constantly seeks out challenges and adventures, and we wonder whether he might run off and join the circus.

Kate learns to jump off furniture and maneuver around child-proof barriers. When Heather and David complain that Kate gets into their rooms, we put hooks high on the doors, to prevent Kate's entry. But Kate figures out how to climb on a chair and engage the hook, locking David in his room.

We try to stay ahead of the children. When that doesn't work, we try to keep up–or catch up.

CHAPTER 4.

Family is extremely important. Work is very important. But Arden and I feel that our lives will be incomplete, unless we also involve ourselves in the community. Arden and I both do this.

Springfield is filled with volunteer opportunities, as people try to make it a good place to live. I join the Planned Parenthood Board, then the Urban League Board, serving for more than a decade as Secretary, Treasurer, Vice Chair and Chair. The Urban League is an outstanding program, administering more than $10 million in grants, serving community needs: early childhood, Head Start, financial counseling, affordable housing, tutoring, tuition assistance, health care, employment counseling and programs for seniors.

For the Urban League, I serve on a group that looks at "achievement gaps" in our schools. We issue a report that documents that too many children of color and too many children eligible for school lunch programs have not been doing well over the years and are not doing well now. The school district knows this, but does not let the public know this, so we issue this report. The school district does not follow up.

I lead an Urban League group that builds affordable housing. We train people in the construction trades, repair houses, arrange subsidies, and rebuild several of Springfield's most challenged neighborhoods. I serve on the Urban League's Head Start committee, enjoying this because of my Head Start experience in Mississippi in 1965. And I read with students in the Urban League's summer Freedom School, enjoying this because of my Freedom School experience in 1965.

I go to a National Urban League conference in Chicago, to hear from Vice President Joe Biden. And the National Urban League introduces me to their Equality Index, comparing African American and white statistics for health, education, employment and civic engagement. This Index is about 70% to 75%, and is not moving forward. This troubles me.

Our lives and our work go well. And we give back to the community in many ways.

CHAPTER 5.

In 1989, it's the centennial of the Johnstown flood. My Grandpa Jack survives this flood, and tells me about it several times when I am young. So our extended family, 31 of us, Mom, Dad, Arden, Kate, Steve, Jane, uncles, aunts, cousins and children, meet together with many others to commemorate this tragic event. We learn the story again: wealthy people build and expand a private recreational lake, putting an earth dam in a narrow valley; a substantial rain breaks down the earth dam, and a flood rushes down the narrow valley and into the town; water rises thirty feet, breaking houses loose;

Grandpa's house floats downriver, with his family on the roof; his brother slips into the water, and Grandpa rescues him; and our family survives, but well over 2,000 people perish.

At a commemorative dinner, David McCullough, the famous historian, speaks. His first book is about this Johnstown flood. Others speak as well, and we meet some survivors, now over 100 years old. We locate our great-grandfather Daniel Kramer's store and the house that the family rebuilds after the flood, and I come away with a much deeper appreciation of this tragic story.

Arden and I also connect to Lincoln's extensive history in our area. As soon as we settle in Springfield, I read Paul Angle's "Here I Have Lived," the history of Lincoln's years there. We meet Harlington Wood, who plays Lincoln in local theater; he is a local attorney who becomes a leader in the United States Department of Justice, going to Wounded Knee and negotiating peace among Native American insurgents, their tribes, and the United States. His extraordinary history, described in his wonderful book, "An Unmarked Journey: The Odyssey of a Federal Judge," takes him to becoming United States Attorney, then District Judge, then Court of Appeals Judge, and he serves as a thoughtful and considerate role model and friend for so many in the community.

CHAPTER 6.

Heather, David and Kate thrive. Heather continues to be a top student, and her fellow students choose her to give the keynote speech at high school graduation; she asks her generation to come together and solve problems throughout the world. David does well also, and his fellow students choose him to be class president. Kate follows my path, mixing school with mischief, doing well at both.

I coach Kate's recreational soccer team, and my message is "play hard, have fun." We win the championship four consecutive years. Kate is our best goalie; this keeps her stationary and comfortable when it is warm, but leaves her exposed when the weather turns cold. One year, it's about ten degrees, snowing and windy for the championship game, and parents watch from their cars. At the end of regulation time, there is no score. As we huddle before overtime, Kate says, "I cannot feel anything in my entire body, except where it hurts." I respond, "You're our goalie. We need you. You have to play." She does, and we play double overtime, until the officials finally declare a scoreless tie. Driving home, Kate is silent–and not happy with me. I say, "That was your coach speaking. Now I'm back to being your Dad." We begin to talk again.

Heather would like a college that features rock concerts, but chooses Harvard. David chooses Cornell. And Kate, after two years at our local community college, chooses

Wisconsin. I advise Kate, when dropping her off at college, to "read a book, have fun."

Each child becomes a serious student, while figuring out how to have fun at the same time. Arden and I are proud and delighted to see each child becoming a decent and responsible adult. We love them so dearly, and we enjoy them as well.

CHAPTER 7.

In early 1996, Dad becomes ill, shortly before Mom and Dad move from their Florida home to a retirement community near Steve and Jane. That spring, Kate has her bat mitzvah, a wonderful family occasion. In my remarks at the bat mitzvah, knowing that Dad is not well, I include the 23rd Psalm: "The Lord is my Shepherd, I shall not want....Yea, though I walk through the valley of the shadow of death, I will fear no evil, for thou art with me." That summer, we learn that Dad is passing from us, and we spend as much time as we can with him. In late August, he passes away.

I speak at the funeral. It's not easy. In the prior section, I include what I say.

In that same summer, 1996, Arden's Mother Millie has a serious heart operation, a multiple bypass. She experiences a full month of coma, then awakens, goes to rehab, gets on a treadmill, and makes a remarkable recovery, living many more years—always setting an extraordinary example. In

2003, Millie has a wonderful 90th birthday, as "Thoroughly Modern Millie." A few years later, she relocates to our house for more care and attention. Arden is wonderful with her mother, and I do my best as well, cooking our secret favorite, hot dogs and beans, when Arden isn't home. After several good years, Millie finally needs full-time attention and moves to a nursing home. She has a wonderful 100th birthday party, surrounded by family and friends, and passes away quietly the next year.

CHAPTER 8.

Work continues to go well. In 1994, I go to a conference on the False Claims Act, a statute that dates back to the Civil War, imposing civil damages whenever a supplier provides "shoddy" goods to the military. The Act, revised in 1986, imposes multiple damages whenever there is a knowingly false monetary claim to the government.

After the conference, I sit down with the Medicaid Fraud Control Unit, which investigates claims from medical care providers to the federal-state Medicaid program. We find some psychiatrists who assert that they provide more hours of care than exist in a day or that a quick check of nursing home medication is really extensive psychotherapy. We also find some dentists, hospitals and pharmacies with a pattern of false claims. As our work increases, I get money from the Department of Justice for an additional attorney and an investigator, and we become part of a multi-agency federal-state task force. We work to recover sufficient damages, usually twice the false charges, in order to deter future fraud, and we require a formal compliance program with training on proper billing practices, in order to ensure that future claims will be legitimate. We expect honest payment for honest service, and we protect the honest billers from unfair competition. Our work makes a difference.

A few years later, I go to a conference about the Americans with Disability Act (ADA), ensuring that people with physical or mental limitations get a full opportunity to enjoy public services and public opportunities. After the conference, I sit down with people from the Springfield Center for Independent Living, particularly Pete Roberts and Starla Norris, to examine whether our community is fully accessible. We begin with the State Capitol, a giant building that houses the Governor, the Legislature, and a great many offices. It's about 100 years old and not fully accessible, so we arrange for an ADA-trained architect to come from the Department of Justice, examine the entire building, and prepare a complete report. I give this report to representatives of the Governor, Legislature, Secretary of State, and Architect of the Capitol, and I ask them two questions: "Do you wish to follow the law?" and "Do you wish to have an accessible public building?" We reach an agreement for immediate removal of all significant barriers as well as future removal of each remaining barrier, as the State renovates the Capitol.

We examine access to local buses, government buildings, the State Fairgrounds, the University of Illinois in Springfield, and many stores and restaurants. When we investigate, we prepare a formal report with photographs, measurements and citations to specific rules and regulations. We then communicate our findings and ask our two questions: "Do you wish to follow the law?" and "Do you wish to have an accessible building?" People always answer "yes," and we work with them to ensure compliance. This is important work. It ensures that our communities are properly open to all. It makes a difference.

CHAPTER 9.

In 2000, at age 60, I realize that I need to become more active, and I start to walk and run a bit in the mornings. After a while, I enter races with the Springfield Runners Club. In 2001, I finish last–but happy–after a ten kilometer run at the conclusion of the State Fair. By 2002, I train for a marathon, running several times a week, increasing my distance and determination. Then I go to Chicago with several friends who also run, and I complete the marathon in less than five hours, losing a toenail in the process. I'm hooked. It's a strange pastime, lonesome yet healthy, offering plenty of time to think. I enter more and more races, do better and better within my age group, and run a marathon every year, including the St. Louis marathon in 2008 and the New York marathon in late October 2009.

For New York, I get up at 4 am, ride with my nephew Jon to a bus, take the bus to the start area, sit for two hours, then head off in a crowd of perhaps 45,000 across the Verrazano Bridge from Staten Island–where I teach after college–to Brooklyn–where Mom, Dad and Steve are born. There is a strong and cold wind, so going up the bridge is difficult, but running down and off the bridge is easy, leading into a flat and lengthy run through Brooklyn. Every thirty minutes, I chew and swallow a "sports bean" full of sugar, caffeine and electrolytes, until the effect–the "buzz"–becomes too strong. We leave Brooklyn, enter Queens, and go up and over another difficult bridge into Manhattan, for a long run up First Avenue, into the Bronx, almost to Yankee Stadium. We turn back into Manhattan for four miles along Fifth Avenue and into Central Park, across 59th Street for the final mile, then a short section back into Central Park to the finish line, still buzzing from sugar and caffeine. I connect with Arden and Jane, return to Steve and Jane's house, shower, have dinner and watch the Yankees defeat the Phillies in the World Series, late into that night. When the buzz finally wears off, I go to sleep. It's a great day, and also the end of my marathon running. I develop plantar fasciitis, heel problems that can come with running, and, as we will soon see, I take on a job with longer hours in 2010, making it difficult to maintain training.

CHAPTER 10.

In October, 2005, I receive a letter from Frontiers International in Springfield, inviting me to keynote their Martin

Luther King Day breakfast in January 2006. Their past speakers include Rosa Parks of the Montgomery Bus Boycott, James Farmer of the Congress of Racial Equality, and Morris Dees of the Southern Poverty Law Center. I'm honored to be their choice–and truly shaken by the responsibility.

I discuss this speech with Guyot, Harry and Armand when we're together in Mississippi in late 2005, and I work on it almost every day. On the day of the speech, I wake at 4 am, go to the office, make a few final changes, complete the speech to my satisfaction, and walk over to the breakfast. Senator Richard L. Durbin speaks briefly before me, and points out that Dr. King was an agitator, telling the truth about injustice that agitated him and should agitate us all.

I rise and speak. It's what I want to say, about Mississippi and Springfield: "I'd like to talk with you this morning about the people in Mississippi who worked to tear down the walls of segregation, and I'd like to talk with you about some work we need to do on some walls in Springfield." I take a deep breath, the audience takes a deep breath, and we go forward. "In community after community across the South, people came together and organized, in order to choose a better future and to create a better future....It was my privilege to help the thousands of civil rights protestors and the parents and the college students and the children, and to help open up the schools and voting and full citizenship for everyone....I've seen the power of community organization in Springfield; I've seen people come together, for schools and churches and for the hundreds of service organizations in this community; so I say, organize yourself, your family, your neighbors, your friends...because this work, this hard work, will actually set you free, will set those around you free, will set this community free, and we need to be free." I go on to speak of "parent-child-teacher-community partnerships that work to see that each child will get the most out of school,...so that the children will want to grow up to be teachers and business-people and public servants for the next generation," and I speak of health-care opportunity and full and equal economic opportunity and justice throughout the community. I repeat several times, "We can do this." The audience rises and applauds.

Two years later, in 2008, the mayor forms a commission to acknowledge the centennial of the 1908 Springfield Race Riot, when a white mob destroys the African American community and lynches two African American businessmen, Scott Burton and William Donnegan. I serve on this commission and create a trial reenactment based on the actual trial for the murder of William Donnegan. This reenactment is called "Mob, Murder, Justice–You Be the Jury," and this draws a 250-person audience, silent and attentive.

In 2009, my friend Lawrence Guyot, former Chair of the Mississippi Freedom Democratic Party, comes to keynote Frontiers International's Martin Luther King Day breakfast. Frontiers asks me to introduce him. Guyot and I talk quietly just before the speech, and I confide that I am applying to become the next United States Attorney, but this is not public information. Guyot believes that "information is power," and he begins his speech by telling the audience that Jim Lewis would like to be the next United States Attorney, and that the audience should support this.

CHAPTER 11.

In fall 2008, it appears that our Senator, Barack Obama, is likely to become our next President. A good friend calls me and leads the conversation to the question of the next United States Attorney. We discuss several possibilities. It dawns on me that I would be a good possibility. Soon after the 2008 election, I write Senator Durbin, outline my priorities, and ask to be considered.

In early 2009, I visit a local attorney and ask for his support. He tells me that he will lead the citizens' committee that will review the applicants and make recommendations to Senator Durbin. I interview with this citizens' committee, and we enjoy an hour of excellent discussion. A month later, Senator Durbin asks me to come for an interview.

I've always appreciated Senator Durbin's extraordinary understanding and advocacy on a wide range of local, national and international issues. We have an excellent discussion, beginning with music theory–our son David's field–and working our way to our concerns about criminal justice. I leave this interview even more appreciative. Then there are months of silence.

In late 2009, I get a package at the office. It contains the forms to fill out, before the FBI investigates you and the President nominates you. I am, it appears, the choice.

6

SPRINGFIELD (2010-2022)

CHAPTER 1.

In early 2010, the Department of Justice asks me to come and meet with representatives of the White House and the Executive Office for United States Attorneys (EOUSA), as well as other officials. Several attorneys quiz me for an hour, to be sure that there's no impediment to my nomination. Then they send me upstairs to meet Attorney General Eric Holder.

I sit in the Attorney General's conference room, the office once used by Robert Kennedy, with Kennedy's portrait looking down at me. Yes, I'm in awe, but I focus on being present and attentive as the Attorney General enters the room. I hand him a monograph describing Springfield's 1908 race riot, because he has just given a speech connecting this 1908 race riot to the formation of the National Association for the

Advancement of Colored People in 1909. When Attorney General Holder says, "I'm looking forward to working with you," it finally hits me: this is actually happening.

In spring 2010, President Obama sends my nomination to the Senate. I fill out lengthy forms for the Senate, then wait. On June 21, 2010, I get a phone call from aides to the Chairman and Ranking Member of the Judiciary Committee, asking about some minor discrepancies in the many forms that I fill out for the FBI and the Senate. I worry that Senate approval might be at risk, due to these discrepancies.

The very next day, June 22, I get another phone call, to my surprise: "The Senate has approved you. Go get sworn in." I arrange for United States District Judge Jeanne Scott to administer the oath of office, I sign a letter of resignation as Assistant United States Attorney, and I use the office intercom to invite people to come to the courtroom. Judge Scott swears me in. It's real. It's official. I am the United States Attorney for the Central District of Illinois. I say to myself, "If you take the job, do the job." I can–and must–help others.

One month later, we have a ceremonial oath at the Old State Capitol, in the House of Representatives where Lincoln served in the 1840s, where he gave his "House Divided" speech when running for the Senate in 1858, and where he rested before his funeral in 1865. Before the ceremony, Arden and I host a lunch for many friends at Maldaner's Restaurant, and some old and dear friends–David Holtzman from Yale and Armand Derfner and Martha Bergmark from Mississippi–speak briefly. Then we head to the Old State Capitol. Rabbi Barry Marks and Dr. Wesley Robinson-McNeece speak about justice, Senator Durbin offers remarks, then Chief United States District Judge Michael McCuskey leads me through the oath of office. I thank just about everybody, beginning with Mom–she's present–and I commit that our Office will do "the right thing, in the right way, for the right reasons."

The Department provides two orientations. The first is an intense three-day introduction in Washington. This begins with a two-hour explanation that ensures our attention: as United States Attorney, you are a "temporary employee," and misconduct will get you into "big trouble," requiring prompt resignation. At this orientation, I hear someone say, "Where you sit can determine where you stand," meaning that our new position may bring about new views. But I hope to maintain my basic view that all people–colleagues and others–are welcome to come to the table and bring their views. Yes, I will have added authority, but this comes with added responsibility to listen.

One month later, we have a second orientation, a week at the National Advocacy Center in Columbia, South Carolina, with a broader view of Department policies and purposes. At this orientation, I learn that our Office has the highest percentage of employees who began 25 to 30 years ago and are now eligible to retire. I will have to find capable replacements.

CHAPTER 2.

As soon as I'm sworn in, we confront a spike in gun violence in Peoria, with 17 gun deaths in the first half of the year. The Police Department responds with saturation patrols throughout the most dangerous neighborhoods, and this serves the immediate purpose, reducing the violence. But saturation cannot be maintained, because this requires too many officers, and the community will begin to resist if this continues too long and becomes an "occupation."

We need longer-term answers. I seek help from the federal Bureau of Alcohol, Tobacco and Firearms, and they send undercover agents to disrupt gun trafficking. And a wise friend, Assistant United States Attorney Tate Chambers, with two years of experience as the national anti-violence coordinator at the Department of Justice, suggests that we discuss a "Don't Shoot" program with Mayor Jim Ardis and local leaders.

"Don't Shoot" is the best available police-community solution, when gangs or groups cause gun violence. David Kennedy, author of the book "Don't Shoot" and Chair of the National Network of Safe Communities, defines "Don't Shoot" as "focused deterrence," meaning that law enforcement works with the community to prosecute the primary people who drive the gun violence, while also reaching out with the community to focus on and deter those who appear most likely to turn to violence in the near future. Across this country, research and experience show that when you prosecute the people who are the primary causes of violence, others will step up to violence–unless you provide effective outreach and deterrence for those who are most likely to step up and use violence.

Peoria adopts David Kennedy's approach. We prosecute two groups of major offenders, and we begin "call-ins" to reach those who appear likely to use violence in the future. At a call-in, selected people, often on probation, are required to attend. They hear messages from Mayor Ardis, from law enforcement–Police Chief, Sheriff, State's Attorney, myself–and from social service providers, victims of violence, former gang members, and voices of faith and conscience. Our law enforcement message is brief, and includes posters on the wall that show people who have been prosecuted and imprisoned. The community message is lengthier and much more effective: "We know you, we care about you, we are concerned for you and for the people you might injure, we will not accept gun violence, we will seek prosecution if there is any gun violence, you must stop, and we will help you–if you stop. Don't shoot." I particularly remember one community representative, expressing her grief for her murdered brother–and also recognizing the devastation within the family of the man who killed her brother. And I certainly remember "G-Rock," a former Gangster Disciple, summarizing his life's journey through many juvenile and adult institutions, and letting the young men (and occasional woman) know that he eventually wakes up, realizes that destruction is not the best way forward, and manages to find a much better life.

In Peoria–and across this country–this approach works. Peoria has a significant reduction in gun violence, thanks to hard work by the Police Department, Mayor Ardis, Sheriff McCoy, State's Attorney Jerry Brady, federal law enforcement, our Office–and community representatives from Peoria Community Against Violence.

Once "Don't Shoot" begins to work, I reach out to the United States Attorneys in the Northern and Southern Districts of Illinois, and we present a joint training on gun violence reduction in September 2013, inviting law enforcement and community leaders from across the state. The Southern District talks about gun violence reduction in East St. Louis, the Central District presents a panel discussion by the Peoria leaders, and the Northern District demonstrates how they do call-ins. To pull it all together, David Kennedy comes, keynotes and comments. This provides state-wide education about reducing gun violence, trying to see that people are not shot, families are not harmed, and potential shooters don't end up in prison.

Peoria gets help from High Point, North Carolina. In High Point, "Don't Shoot" significantly reduces gun violence, allowing children to play outside safely and enabling people to walk to church without fear. Peoria leaders go to High Point, and High Point leaders come to Peoria, working together to reduce violence and fear. Whenever I speak, I deliver the simple message that I learn from High Point: we seek communities where children can play outside and parents can sleep through the night without fear. I begin to hear more and more people who deliver the same simple message.

After a few years of "Don't Shoot," I come across an analysis of gun violence in Wilmington, Delaware. At Wilmington's request, the Center for Disease Control analyzes six years of shooting. This analysis indicates that people who shoot other people almost always have damage in their own past, whether abuse as children, serious struggles during schooling, gun injury or other damage. I turn this analysis into a power-point presentation and provide it to leaders in gun violence reduction efforts across central Illinois, to help people understand that–as others say–"damaged people damage people," "hurt people hurt people." This CDC analysis concludes that we need increased effort to reduce abuse to children, struggles during schooling and other gun injuries, in a community-wide effort to reduce damage, before damage leads to further damage.

As years go by, I talk with several people who cause terrible damage to others when young, who receive lengthy terms of imprisonment, and who "age out" of their confusion, anger, despair and violence. I support "Don't Shoot" as an effort to save lives and reduce damage, but I also learn that we need to invest more time and effort in young people before they become involved in confusion, anger, despair, damage and violence.

Carl Cannon, an immensely-respected community leader in Peoria, is part of our "Don't Shoot" work, serving as the final community speaker at each call-in. Carl also involves us all in "Don't Start," his effort to intervene before damage to young people. Carl's effort includes intervention in several troubled schools, with support from the school district, as well as intervention with people returning from prison, to help them get back on track.

I work alongside Carl for years while I am United States Attorney, and we continue after I retire. In 2021, the Peoria school district asks Carl to take 30 students who have not completed eighth grade successfully and who are likely to be lost to the streets, and Carl puts these students, with full support from their families, through an intensive summer school, with mentors–"gamechangers"–who have been on the streets and in the prisons and can now reach these young people effectively. Carl and his gamechangers will continue to work with these young people and their families, as the students enter high school.

Carl asks me to speak at this summer school graduation. What should I say? I talk to these young people about other young people, Freedom School students in McComb in 1965, who respond to difficult circumstances, finding a way when there seemed not to be a way.   These young people in Peoria can do this too.

In Mississippi, I see people who head directly to help others in trouble. In Peoria, I see Carl and his colleagues head directly to help others in trouble. If we learn to do this in all our communities, we will do so much good and avoid so much damage.

For me, Carl is another "life teacher." I recommend Carl's memoir, "Full Cannon."

CHAPTER 3.

Attorney General Holder suggests a nation-wide emphasis on officer safety, and I begin this work alongside our Law Enforcement Coordinator, Terry Lucas. Working with the Northern and Southern Districts, we bring together approximately 80 law enforcement leaders for a one-day meeting in our Office to define and address issues that require attention. We identify 17 specific officer safety issues, we get to work, and we update the law enforcement community as we make some progress.

We take a particularly close look at the "Below 100" program, offering effective safety training. More than 100 law enforcement officers die in accidents and shootings each year; approximately half of these deaths could be prevented; and the premise of "Below 100" is that we have the obligation to prevent that which is preventable, through additional and repeated safety training, emphasis on safe driving, and increased attention to physical and mental health and wellness, in order to bring the deaths "Below 100." I go to "Below 100" training alongside law enforcement officers, then we begin this work. There is much to do, if we wish to have officers who are safe, within communities that are also safe. The police and the community share a common goal: safety and peace.

I regularly attend breakfasts, lunches, dinners, trainings and meetings with law enforcement across the District, speaking many times about our mutual concerns: violence reduction, officer safety, public safety. At these meertings, I give out wallet-size cards that simply say "Seriously?" and these become very popular with law enforcement.

CHAPTER 4.

I sign up for the Office Management and Budget Subcommittee (OMB), which provides support and advice to the Attorney General's Advisory Committee (AGAC) and EOUSA on significant operational and financial issues. After a few years, AGAC and EOUSA ask me to become Chair of OMB, just as the federal "sequester" kicks in, shrinking every military and civilian budget. My first task is to convene and lead a two-day meeting in Washington, in order to plan the reduction of $130 million–approximately 7%–from the $1.9 billion budget for United States Attorney's Offices. With a dozen United States Attorneys, assisted by the EOUSA

Director and staff, we go through approximately 360 line items in the budget, looking for potential savings that will still allow us to maintain our workforce and serve our purpose. We find that we can survive for a short while, if we postpone some technological improvements and reduce some other expenses. I put our specific suggestions into an eight-page item-by-item report and send this to AGAC, then I spend two days explaining this at an AGAC meeting, leading them toward our recommendations.

This process exposes some differences within our leadership. I try–but fail–to resolve these differences. I don't wish to lead a "house divided," so I step down as OMB chair. And then our effort turns out to be unnecessary. Senator Patti Murray from Washington and Representative Paul Ryan from Wisconsin bring the Senate and House into a budget agreement that does not require the 7% cut, and EOUSA receives the full $1.9 billion budget.

EOUSA allows a United States Attorney's Office to hire attorneys and support staff whenever there is enough money in the budget allotted to the Office. But before any hiring, EOUSA also holds back 5% at the beginning of each fiscal year, for special and unforeseen expenses. Because I understand EOUSA's budget process, I realize that this 5% makes partial–not complete–sense. EOUSA slowly releases half of this–2.5%–to our Offices as the year progresses, but EOUSA also holds the other half–2.5%–without any specific need or a use for the money. Within OMB, I argue that our Offices should have this second 2.5%, and my argument makes sense, but I'm not a leader any longer, so few listen, and my argument fails.

This additional resource, 2.5% of all Office budgets, would be almost $50 million nation-wide, and would be extremely welcome. For our Office, our 2.5% would have added an attorney to address violence as well as additional support staff in our branch offices. This money, already appropriated by Congress, should actually reach our Offices.

CHAPTER 5.

I understand community organizing, so I do community outreach that addresses legal concerns. Illinois Attorney General Lisa Madigan and I bring communities and law enforcement together in two large public meetings, one in Peoria and one in Urbana, on issues of hate crimes and bullying. I follow this up with work on Springfield's anti-bullying effort in schools and throughout the community.

I also speak at a community meeting to commemorate the Civil Rights Act of 1964, a law that redefines our country's approach to the issue of race, on July 2, 2014, the anniversary of the law, in the Old State Capitol, in the Chamber where Lincoln served. And Lincoln–actually a Lincoln reenactor, Randy Duncan–is there. I look over at Lincoln–Duncan–and explain how this country got from 1865 to 1964, then I explain the significance of the Civil Rights Act. On another occasion, commemorating the 150th anniversary of Lincoln's funeral, I speak again, this time at St. Paul's Episcopal Cathedral, about our journey from 1865 to the present.

Like many colleagues across the country, I reach out to Islamic communities, visiting mosques in Urbana, Springfield, Peoria and Bloomington. I don't want the Islamic community to be targeted or bullied, if I can do something. So we meet, we get to know each other, we share hospitality, we discuss security, and I let them know that I will come when they need me and whenever they simply would enjoy a visit. I meet some wonderful people and gain some friends.

In Peoria, the mosque shares a parking lot with an evangelical church. The Imam and the Minister become friends, and they also become friends with the local Rabbi. Once they are friends, they introduce their congregations to each other. Then they put together a book and film: "No Joke." One evening, they are watching a baseball game; the Minister and Rabbi are explaining the rules to the Imam; and the Rabbi's wife comes in and asks, "Is this a joke?" This gives them their title. Their book and film explore the altogether human dimension of getting to know, respect and appreciate each other, and I use this film in a course that I later teach.

In 2016, in response to some anti-Islamic political rhetoric, the Peoria mosque holds a meeting for the entire community, Islamic, Christian and Jewish, and 700 people attend. Mayor Ardis, state and local representatives and religious leaders speak, and I speak as well. I say that the best response to a bad idea–anti-Islamic rhetoric–is a better idea, and that the entire Peoria community, represented in this mosque on this evening, has a much better idea: we must care for each other, in good and not-so-good times.

Much of my work involves connecting with people and communities on issues of concern, always with the goals of understanding, peace and safety. I particularly enjoy this work.

CHAPTER 6.

After a few years, Attorney General Holder introduces "Smart on Crime," in an effort to improve our criminal justice system. Beginning in the 1980s, our country relies on mass incarceration as the answer to every problem, so that we have many more people in prison, in absolute numbers and percentage, than any other country. We have been making a mistake. We do not need to use the hammer of imprisonment with so many people. We have other tools to encourage people to behave properly toward each other.

Therefore, we explore alternatives to imprisonment. For many years, our Peoria Office has a pre-trial program that offers an alternative to prison for non-violent drug offenders who are trapped in their own addiction. This program involves in-patient or out-patient rehabilitation, extensive support and supervision from federal probation officers, and monthly meetings as a group with prosecutors, defense attorneys and a federal judge. About 90% of the people succeed and graduate back to family and employment. This restores lives and families–and saves a lot of money, since imprisonment is so expensive.

One November, Attorney General Holder comes to Peoria, participates in the program's monthly meeting, and listens as one person, flanked by his wife and children, graduates from the program and thanks his fellow participants and the court. The Attorney General promotes this as a model for other courts. And the Attorney General expresses his appreciation, when United States Attorneys reserve incarceration for the most serious offenses, and the federal prison population begins to decrease.

When Attorney General Holder comes, he also meets with people in our Office and with the leaders of the "Don't Shoot" program. He makes a particular connection with Carl Cannon, and they keep in touch.

"Smart on Crime" distributes $15 million in resources. We compete for a share of these resources, based on our existing programs, such as "Don't Shoot" and pre-trial diversion for non-violent drug offenders, as well as our efforts to assist former prisoners in their reentry into their communities. We receive money for an attorney and a reentry specialist, and we begin a monthly district-wide meeting for everyone interested in "Smart on Crime."

I visit the new Warden at the nearby federal prison, FCI Pekin, and we talk for an hour about improving success for people when they leave prison. The Warden does not want people to return to prison, and we don't want to prosecute someone for yet another crime. How can we improve success? After we talk, the Warden takes me around the prison, showing me the education and counseling that is directed to improving peoples' chances. I meet the reentry coordinator and participate in training for reentry, including a mock exercise that simulates the first month after prison. I go through this exercise alongside prisoners, and I don't do well with the many demands and requirements. I fail a few (mock) drug tests and run out of food and money, ending up back in prison.

Reentry is difficult, in the exercise and in the real world. Every community should support efforts to increase successful reentry, since this helps people, assists families and neighborhoods, reduces crime, reduces re-imprisonment–and saves money. If we become "Smart on Crime," we can increase what is good and reduce what is harmful.

CHAPTER 7.

We have illegal drugs in our communities, and these cause significant damage. At first, our Office focuses on people who cook and distribute large amounts of methamphetamine. We train state and local officers on federal conspiracy investigations, and this leads to prosecutions of numerous methamphetamine cooks and accomplices, greatly reducing this problem.

But a new problem emerges: opiates. In our country, we consume most of the opiates in the world. If we restrict prescription opiates, many people turn to heroin and fentanyl. It's cheap and available–and often lethal. The toll rises rapidly, becoming an epidemic, surpassing guns and automobiles as a cause of death.

What can we do? Prosecution is often appropriate but is not fully effective, even for heroin dealers and those who cause death, because heroin sales involve small amounts and less-organized groups. Addiction treatment can help, but is not always available. So education and prevention become critical.

I go to a two-day training presented by the Mayo Clinic in Minneapolis, and we develop a community education program in Peoria, again with Mayor Ardis, Sheriff McCoy, the Police Chief, the State's Attorney and other leaders. We attend two hours of training alongside 100 doctors in Peoria, to ensure that we all understand the risks of prescription drugs and the dangers of heroin and fentanyl. For the community as a whole, we hold a series of public meetings that feature a recovering heroin addict who describes the difficult struggle. We bring Sam Quinones to Peoria, to talk about his extraordinary book, "Dreamland: The True Tale of America's

Opiate Epidemic." We show "Chasing the Dragon," a short film of young people talking about their desperate struggles with heroin addiction. We use education as the basis for prevention, and I write an article about Peoria's community education for the United States Attorney's Bulletin, putting our message out across the country.

This work–education, prevention and treatment, backed by law enforcement as needed–will go on for quite a while, as long as this terrible epidemic continues. We need to make some headway against this epidemic. In retirement, I volunteer with the county Department of Public Health, helping with a community effort toward education, prevention and treatment. It's important.

Many drug crimes are subject to "mandatory minimum" sentences. In our Office, an attorney submits a written request for authority to prosecute, including a section on any potential mandatory minimum. After a few years, I'm asked about our use of these mandatory minimum sentences. Yes, we follow the law as written, but we apparently ask for more such sentences than other districts. I ask a person in the Department about comparative statistics and practices, but he has no information. Years later, I learn that the Sentencing Commission, an independent body, may have information that compares districts. And now, with hindsight, I see that we should have looked more closely and been more selective when seeking mandatory minimum sentences, because following the letter–and not the intent–of the law can become overly punitive, and we should not allow this to happen.

We make this mistake. I should not allow this to happen.

CHAPTER 8.

Our Office also works on public corruption. In Illinois, some political leaders have a "pay-to-play" approach to state government, favoring those who contribute to campaigns. Illinois does limited monitoring of state grants to favored donors, and public money is too often diverted into private pockets. So we bring and continue a series of grant investigations, successfully prosecuting a number of officials and grantees, until the state improves its grant practices and its monitoring. This reduces corruption.

An investigation reveals that a member of Congress, Aaron Schock, uses public money for private purposes. A grand jury charges him for approximately $150,000 of fraudulent claims and expenditures. After I retire, this prosecution is assigned to a different United States Attorney's Office in a different District, and this case is resolved with a plea that represents a compromise.

CHAPTER 9.

On August 9, 2014, a young white police officer, Darren Wilson, shoots and kills a young African American man,

Michael Brown, in Ferguson, Missouri. Across this country, this tragic event causes people to reexamine the questions of police, community, force and race.

I decide to push for better answers, and I begin by looking closely at standards for use of lethal force. The FBI standard, for example, is that "agents may use deadly force only when necessary–when the agent has a reasonable belief that the subject of such force poses an imminent danger of death or serious physical injury to the agent or another person." To ensure compliance with this standard, the FBI trains and retrains in "judgmental shooting," the proper use of lethal force. I take this training–simulations with an electronic gun–so that I will know what I am talking about. I have to make split-second decisions–and I'm hesitant to shoot. Is there imminent and significant danger? What do I believe, under the specific circumstances, and is my belief reasonable? It is extremely difficult to make quick decisions with lethal consequences.

Based on this training, I have a complex message: the legal authority is broad and general, partially objective, partially subjective; this authority contains significant limits, requiring genuine danger and genuine belief; and for officers, there must be training and retraining, good judgment and truly objective review of that judgment. Training on "judgmental shooting" must include training that will help an officer step back, deescalate and decide not to shoot unless absolutely necessary. I try to clarify this complexity whenever I speak to law enforcement or the community.

I read two reports from the Department of Justice about Ferguson. The first report, 80 pages, analyzes the specific shooting in great detail and concludes that Michael Brown appears to move back toward the officer in a manner that could support a reasonable belief of imminent and significant danger. Based on this conclusion, the Department decides not to prosecute the officer.

Let's understand this conclusion: when there's sufficient evidence of a struggle with an officer, moving well away, then turning, moving back, and beginning to get close, an officer can lawfully choose force. But the officer has another choice: the officer can disengage, because force can mean serious injury or death. Force is allowed, not required. A friend with significant experience in law enforcement tells me that the officer should have disengaged and called for support, and I agree.

The second Ferguson report, more than 100 pages, examines criminal justice, concluding that Ferguson directs its officers to focus not on legitimate law enforcement but instead on collecting more and more money through fines and fees from residents. This alienates law enforcement from the community, destroying trust, bringing injustice instead of justice. In retirement, I use this report when I teach a course in Race and Inequality.

Lethal force is part of a much larger issue: modern policing. President Obama appoints a commission to re-set expectations for 21st century policing, and I read the report and include it in my messages to law enforcement and the community. Two members of this commission, Tracey Meares of Yale Law School and Sean Smoot of the Illinois Police Benevolent and Protective Association, have Springfield connections, and I bring them together in our Office with law enforcement and community leaders, for a discussion of the way forward to better practices, better policing, and community support.

And I participate in community meetings about policing. Both NOBLE–National Organization of Black Law Enforcement Executives–and the FBI develop training materials for the community, so that police and the community will know what to expect from each other. These materials and meetings include information about traffic stops and street encounters, since many people share this experience. We try to answer the questions: what can officers do, what can people do, so that this experience ends properly and peacefully? I get a lot more education on police-community problem-solving, and I try to share this education with others.

In Mississippi, I learn to be concerned about economic, political and educational opportunity and social justice. As United States Attorney, I learn to add criminal justice and police-community problem-solving to my list of unresolved concerns.

CHAPTER 10.

Police-community problem-solving can make a real difference, when it works. Problems can be properly addressed and even solved, if law enforcement and the community can find ways to work with each other, rather than having law enforcement with limited community support or a community with limited law enforcement support. Yes, police and the community have significant differences in their culture and role, but these differences–and the apprehensions that police and the community have about each other–might be bridged in part, if there is some effort.

As United States Attorney, I review several thousand federal prosecutions that result in imprisonment, so I appreciate that crimes do real damage to real people, to property and to the sense of trust and safety that we expect and need in our daily lives. How should we respond to crime? We know from experience that responding to crime with an automatic determination to punish and incarcerate is excessive, ineffective, inhumane and counter-productive, causing further damage, so we are now trying to measure our responses.

Who decides on the measures and the responses? It should not be law enforcement alone or the community alone. Together, they should analyze their problems–whether violence, property crime, drug crime or juvenile crime–in order to define their primary concerns and to figure out how to work together to reduce and eliminate these problems. As United States Attorney, I confront gun violence, drug distribution and white collar property crime as well as imprisonment, and I also work on alternatives to imprisonment and reentry after imprisonment, as well as sponsoring a conference on mental health and the law–so I know that there is an effective police-community strategy for every problem, if people will come together and apply that strategy.

Gun violence? Strategies include focussed deterrence like "Don't Shoot" and community programs to help troubled young people, before they turn toward gun crime. Property crime? Strategies include patrolling high-crime areas and working with stores and neighborhoods to reduce risk. Drug distribution? Strategies include prosecuting dealers, offering treatment to addicted people, and educating the community. Jailing and imprisonment? Strategies include incarceration if necessary and alternatives to incarceration if possible. Results? We must analyze outcomes, to see whether a strategy is effective. Trust? We should expect the police to build–and rebuild–trust with the entire community.

This is not just theory. Instead, it is a realistic path toward protecting people and saving lives, benefitting potential victims of crimes and people who might otherwise commit these crimes. A community should have enough good people, ready to come together and push toward this goal.

This work–all my work–is driven by one belief: that we can increase opportunity and well-being, while decreasing harm. I believe that life is a gift, a mysterious gift; that we must enhance life for people when we can; and that we must free people from harm when we can. Where and when do I begin to have this understanding of our world–and our responsibility within our world: in Mississippi, many years ago.

CHAPTER 11.

United States Attorneys form a strong community. We maintain regular communication, working together through regional groups and subject matter groups, sharing good ideas with each other, and meeting nation-wide once a year, including three extraordinary discussions about justice with President Obama at the White House. I take leadership seriously, knowing that I must always do my best, just to keep up within this special community.

I am the oldest United States Attorney, by several months. I have the longest arrest record, due to my three civil rights arrests in the 1960s in Mississippi. But distinctions do not really matter. We are bound together by common values, we all have strong connections with our communities, and we all try to strengthen police-community problem-solving.

At the very first orientation, the Department of Justice emphasizes that the position of United States Attorney is temporary and that you should prepare for your successor. Every decision should be good for the present and good for the future. So I establish a leadership group for the office, meeting monthly and ensuring that the entire District understands our purposes, our goals, our concerns. I hire well-qualified people, seeking out highly motivated people with diverse life experiences, emphasizing character and judgment. I work to ensure a positive culture–a welcome table–within the office, with fairness and opportunity for all. I do everything that I can to strengthen the District.

In late 2015, our new Attorney General, Loretta Lynch, asks us all to "run through the tape." As a marathoner, I fully understand: the work is important, the time is short, and we must put forth every effort in our final year. So I focus on "Don't Shoot," opiate reduction and criminal justice reform.

In late 2015, together with the Illinois Criminal Justice Information Authority (ICJIA), we put on a two-day state-wide gun violence reduction conference in Peoria, once again with David Kennedy to keynote. ICJIA offers grants to communities that wish to follow up on this work, and the Peoria Police Department offers technical assistance, so "Don't Shoot" begins to take root in other communities. I make many trips to Champaign-Urbana and Quincy, and spend time with the Springfield Mayor and police leaders, as these communities all try to address their gun violence. This "Don't Shoot" idea, bringing law enforcement together with the community for the safety and betterment of all, is taking hold.

CHAPTER 12.

As 2016 begins, I consider retirement. I'm good at this work, but not indispensable. I wake full of energy, but get tired by the end of the day. In June, I let people know that I'll retire in December.

Mom has her 103rd birthday, votes in the 2016 election, and begins to fade away. Arden, David and I visit and talk with her just before Thanksgiving, and she passes away a week later. She is strong, she pursues life in her own way, and–as I say at her interment–she is loved by many, even when she annoys some. For me, I love her and I miss her. I'd like to still be able to talk with Mom and Dad.

I work hard to the very last day, to accomplish as much as possible, and I leave quietly. I retire on Friday, December 24, after six and one-half years as United States Attorney, 39 years with the Department of Justice, and 50 years as an attorney, beginning at less than $1 per hour for LCDC in Mississippi. One week later, Arden and I take off for eight weeks, first to New Mexico to see David, then to California for a wedding, and then to six places in Florida in six weeks. When we return, I put my new life together. I join Arden at the Fit Club, several times a week. I volunteer with the Department of Public Health program to reduce opiate abuse. I continue to be a concerned citizen, just as I have always been.

In spring 2018, Kate and I teach a political science course

on race and inequality at Lincoln Land Community College. We have excellent readings, including Martin Luther King's speech at the 1963 March on Washington, his Letter from a Birmingham Jail, James Baldwin's "The Fire Next Time," and John Dollard's "Caste and Class in a Southern Town," as well as material on Springfield's 1908 Race Riot, the National Urban League's Equality Index, and readings on present-day issues of race, gender and economic class. The students–ages 18 to 70–are enthusiastic, and we have excellent discussions. Kate and I enjoy doing this together. For me, this pulls together everything that I learned from nine years in Mississippi and all the years thereafter. So Kate and I teach the same basic class, with added readings from Frederick Douglass and civil rights workers, at the University of Illinois at Springfield in spring 2020, until class is interrupted by the Covid pandemic.

I continue to be involved in the community, working with immigrant organizations, disability advocates, the African American History Museum, criminal justice reform advocates and others, and speaking frequently at rallies and events. Arden and I travel a lot: multiple trips to Europe and to Hawaii, and many trips to places in between–including Chicago Cub games, win some, lose some. Right now, as I complete the First Edition of this memoir, my primary efforts are immigration advocacy, re-entry and justice reform, the History Museum and teaching. In a few years, I may consider a quieter retirement.

CHAPTER 13.

As I complete the First Edition, I approach and pass birthday number 80. Birthday number 10: I'm in summer camp. Birthday number 20: summer camp as well, but this time I'm a counselor at a camp for children with challenges, appreciating these young people, our similarities, our differences. I hear the song, "Smoke Gets In Your Eyes," and wonder what is ahead. Birthday number 30: I'm in Oxford, Mississippi, running Legal Services, playing bid whist with good friends, enjoying a bit of liquid refreshment. Birthday number 40: Arden comes to Washington, and so do Mom and Dad, so they can meet. Birthday number 50: Mom, Dad, Steve and Jane come to Springfield, and we have dinner at home with a few friends. Birthday number 60: I begin walking and running, becoming a marathon runner for the next decade. Birthday number 70: I've become the United States Attorney, and we've just had a big party for the ceremonial oath-taking. Birthday number 80: due to the risks of coronavirus, we're at home instead of our planned family trip to Iceland; Kate and her wonderful husband Drew come, and we visit in our backyard. These birthdays outline my life, and I appreciate my life.

I always have questions. Have I been, as I ask in my high school research paper, sufficiently independent and "hardened for voyages" or dependent and "softened for encounters?" I've headed into jails, prisons, courtrooms and struggles across this country, trying to help, trying to get it right, while being completely soft-hearted when it comes to family. How about the questions presented by Erik Erikson's writings on psychosocial development, defining eight questions that we confront in the course of our lives: (1) trust versus mistrust, (2) autonomy versus shame and doubt, (3) initiative versus guilt, (4) industry versus inferiority, (5) identity versus role confusion, (6) intimacy versus isolation, (7) generativity versus stagnation, and (8) ego integrity versus despair? I read Erikson on my own while in college, and I try to answer these questions over time, as they arise. I think that I've done fairly well: I do learn trust, thanks to Mom and Dad and Elizabeth and George, who take care of me when I'm young, and thanks to Arden when I mature; I learn autonomy and initiative and industry, and I begin to understand my identity and my role; I am extremely fortunate to have a wonderful family, with Arden, our three children and Drew and grand-children; I continue to be generative; and my life makes sense.

What about my own questions about choice and purpose? Have I made good choices, and redeemed myself after poor choices? Have I served good purposes? I believe that I maintain a reasonably consistent choice and purpose: love the immediate family and care for the larger–and too-often struggling–human family.

How have I done with Cain's question, "Am I my brother's keeper?" I've worked to eliminate all forms of discrimination; these violate our shared humanity. I've tried to help young people. I've worked for religious tolerance. I've fought for the rule of law and the rule of reason, as well as social and economic justice. I've tried to be a good family member, friend and citizen of my community–and the world.

I'm delighted with our children. Heather Esme is a professor at Harvard Law School, running their Legal Aid Bureau, serving people amid economic distress; she has two wonderful sons, Liam and Ollie, both growing into good young people. David is a music professor at the University of New Mexico, specializing in music and neurobiology, playing music, leading a full life. Kate is a lawyer in Albuquerque, happily married to Drew, with a very young, very cute, very lively son. Arden and I love them all dearly.

Is it possible to be comfortable, as we appear to be, within a world that has so much pain, tragedy and struggle? No, it isn't, not really. I am still concerned, uncomfortable, dissatisfied and agitated, just as I've been for more than fifty years, because we continue to live amid so much difficulty as a community, state and nation. We live amid discrimination and poverty; we do not meet our obligation to support and educate our young people; we tolerate injustice; and we waste our potential, allowing our world to stand still or slide back, when we need to come together and push forward.

We can anesthetize ourselves against some of this pain, tragedy and struggle, but only for a while. We have an alternative to anesthesia: we can acknowledge the pain, confront each problem, and work to make it right. Who will do this work, and when? In my office, I have this message: "If not us, who? If not now, when?"

Let's be clear and honest: social justice is a necessity, not an option. If we do not have social justice, we lose trust–and cohesion–and community–and humanity. As Dr. King tells us in his letter from a Birmingham jail, "Injustice anywhere is a threat to justice everywhere….Whatever affects one directly, affects all indirectly." As a people, we need to complete our work, eliminating poverty, discrimination, ignorance and injustice, and then–only then–we will actually become what we pretend to be, "We, the people," living amid genuine opportunity, in "the land of the free and the home of the brave."

I return to Harry Bowie's words, on our way to jail in February 1965: "We must keep pushing. They will keep pushing against us. If we stop, they will win." Pragmatic? Yes. Prophetic? Yes.

CHAPTER 14.

I am thankful for the gift of life, and to friends and companions along the way: David and Bill from college, Peter from law school, Harry and Guyot and Ms. Quin and Wayne Anthony and David and Al and Armand from Mississippi, Gerry and Colin and Kathy and Charlotte from work, and Fred and Terri and others from the community. I am profoundly thankful to Senator Durbin for opening the door to my six years as United States Attorney. And I am profoundly thankful to Sherry Yanow, "sywriter," an author and teacher, for reviewing this memoir and encouraging me to say what I wish to say. Particular thanks to Drew Thompson, who accepted my edits and skillfully turned a manuscript into this book.

I am eternally thankful for my family: Mom and Dad and Elizabeth and George and Steve and Jane, all watching out for me; Heather Esme, David and Kate, teaching me the basics of modern parenting, and entertaining me along the way; our growing family, with Drew, Liam, Ollie and Miles; and Arden, for love and life itself.

NOTE: This memoir is intended for family and friends, and for non-commercial use.

POSTSCRIPT: SPRINGFIELD (2020-2022)

I finish this memoir in 2020, distribute 300 copies of the First Edition, then update and revise it for a Second Edition and again for this Edition.

I serve on the Board of the African American History Museum, helping to tell important stories about families, churches and leaders within the community, as well as nationally-significant stories about Negro League Baseball and about the Springfield Race Riot of 1908–which leads to the formation of the National Association for the Advancement of Colored People. I am working with others on "Rising From The Ashes," a booklet that will accompany the Museum's permanent exhibit about the Riot, describing how the African American community, then the broader community, addresses the devastation and slowly rebuilds the community.

I continue to work with others to help people succeed after imprisonment. Dave Risley, a friend and former colleague in the United States Attorney's Office, and I persuade people to form a Reentry Resource Council, now meeting monthly, bringing more and more resources together. Then I work with Ralph Loewenstein and others to prepare a six-page Reentry Resource Guide to describe the services that are already available in Springfield; this Guide will be distributed to people in prison, people released from imprisonment, and anyone else who might benefit. I work with two formerly imprisoned people to develop an intensive reentry program to serve people with the most difficult struggles, and they connect with East Springfield Community Center Commission and obtain a state grant to support this work. I also help another formerly imprisoned person, Lynard Joiner, to expand his reentry program to serve even more people, and this is gaining significant financial support. And I work within the Jewish Community Relations Council, a group with extraordinary talent, to support these reentry initiatives. These initiatives work: people who participate in these initiatives generally succeed and rarely return to prison, while people who do not participate return to prison more often.

I continue to serve on the Board of the Springfield Immigrant Advocacy Network (SIAN), helping them become a non-profit corporation and obtain funds for community advocacy and service.

Arden continues to be active and purposeful. This includes work with the Springfield Jewish Federation, the Academy of Lifelong Learning, Women Rising, a Hadassah book club, an Anti-Rust women's group, the Compass program for elementary school children who are experiencing difficulty, and many other activities. The pandemic imposes some limits–we are fully vaccinated, fully boosted and fully careful–and we work within these limits.

And I receive a wonderful surprise: the Lincoln the Lawyer award from the Abraham Lincoln Association. Judge Harlington Wood, the "life teacher" for so many, received this award many years ago. I am astounded to be considered in this company.

What should I say, when I receive this award? I borrow directly from the Gettysburg Address: we should rededicate ourselves; we should finish the work; we should resolve that the dead will not have died in vain; we should bring forth a new birth of freedom; and we should ensure that government of the people, by the people, and for the people, will not perish from this earth.

I continue to push toward this goal. Will we approach this goal–or will we allow it to slip away from us? I do not know. But I know that I will continue to hear Harry's voice: "Keep pushing."

POSTSCRIPT: ALBUQUERQUE (2022-2023)

After 38 good years in Springfield, Arden and I decide to move, to be with our children. In late 2021, Kate applies and is chosen to be an Assistant United States Attorney in New Mexico. Soon after, Kate and Drew learn that they're pregnant! They move from St. Louis to Albuquerque (where David teaches) in January 2022, and we follow them in March 2022. On April 3, 2022, Kate delivers Miles Henry Lewis Thompson into this world, into a loving family. Miles enjoys every day, and quickly learns more and more new skills.

Arden and I hike, enjoying trails through the foothills of the Sandia mountains. We both work out with trainers at the Jewish Community Center (JCC). One day at the JCC, I join an older men's group, "OMG," with a very thoughtful facilitator, meeting for 1 1/2 hours each Wednesday. This group has 20 or more men, ages 65-95, each caring and interesting. In this group, we talk about how we're doing and about serious concerns that we share: life, health, experience, struggle, loss, death, gratitude–and not politics. This is a welcome table–I always appreciate welcome tables–where I listen, learn, open up, participate and settle into a new community. I make friends and look forward to each meeting.

In November 2022, I get a nasty surprise. I begin to run out of breath, energy and appetite. My brother Steve tells me–directs me–to go to the emergency room immediately, where they find a partial blockage in a coronary artery. I go to the Heart Hospital, where they insert a catheter into an artery, thread it up to the blockage, and insert three stents. When the doctor finishes, he says, "It's fixed," and I follow doctor's orders and work my way back to full activity. This is the first time that something goes seriously wrong within my body.

In June 2023, I get a much nastier surprise: my dear brother Steve is slipping away. I go east to visit him. Steve is supported by his devoted wife Jane and surrounded by his loving family, but this will be the last time for me to see him and speak with him. A week or so later, Steve passes away peacefully: a wonderful son–brother–husband–father–grandfather–great-grandfather–doctor–friend.

Arden, Esme, Kate, Drew, Miles and I join Steve's family and friends as we all say our final goodbyes. I speak at his funeral: "I rermember a big brother who really knew how to do big things, and I looked up to him and learned from him. I learned how to be a little brother, and that has some valuable lessons: I watched him and learned how to do things right; I learned to listen, particularly to Steve, and I learned to respect his property and his toys and to respect his boundaries." I cry while I speak, and I motion to Arden to come and stand with me, to be ready if I become unable to read what I've written.

With Arden at my side, I make it through to my conclusion: "I was so fortunate to have Steve as my big brother. I already miss him a lot, I will miss him for all my days, and I will love and remember him forever."

One very recent night, I fall asleep while watching "Southside With You"–a movie based on the first day that Barack and Michelle Obama spend together casually, when he's a summer law student and she's his advisor at a law firm–and I have the following dream: I'm a young man sitting with Barack and other young men outside a community center. A young man asks, "What does your family do for Christmas?" I reply, "My Mom does it like the magazines," and I put my right hand on Barack's arm and say, "I know what you'll be doing this Christmas"–meaning that he'll be with Michelle and her family. Then the young man asks, "What are you going to do with your life?" I reply, laughing, "My Mom believes that I should be a corporate lawyer, but not for me, no way." And I wake up–to find that it's a new day, I'm happily retired and in Albuquerque, and Arden is sleeping peacefully at my side.

EPILOGUE

On a family vacation in Utah a few years ago, we–Arden and I, together with our next generation, Heather Esme, David, Kate and Drew, together with their next generation, Liam and Ollie–go river-rafting. Our raft approaches a very low bridge, and the guide sreps out and tells us to get all the way down into the raft. There isn't enough room for all of us, so I must step out as well.

I try to hold on, but the current, cool, swift and strong, takes me away. I float under the low bridge and down the river, feet first, buoyed by my life vest, looking up at the blue sky, smiling. I slowly work my way toward the river bank; another rafting group, resting on shore, extends a paddle; I grab the paddle and reach shore safely. As soon as I float away, David steps out of the raft and swims after me, and we all meet and reassemble on the river bank, then continue down the river.

I am healthy and active now, but my time on earth will come to an end–our time does come to an end. When my time ends, I would hope to step out into a cool current and float down a river, looking up at a blue sky. I would hope to smile at all my good fortune, and I would hope that–as in my childhood prayer–I've done the world some good.

7

POEMS

I am not a poet. Before 2020, I never tried to write a poem. And then, in that extraordinary year, I wrote three poems. "By Candlelight" begins with the Adam and Eve's initiation into knowledge, humanity and mortality–then the poem moves to our own initiation into knowledge, humanity and mortality during the pandemic. "A Moment, Please" follows the arc of my life, born in the midst of a world war, joining the civil rights movement, and finding love. "My Country, Tis of Thee" traces the course from youthful hopefulness through real-world experience toward some wisdom about human existence.

I expect these three to be my last poems, but then–surprise–I write two more: "Srsly" and "Yes, It Is."

Will there be more? I doubt it, but I do like putting my questions about life into poems.

BY CANDLELIGHT (2020)

It begins.
A man and woman
Share an apple,
Enjoy the pulp
And the juice,
And fall to earth.

In 2019, it begins anew.
A virus shifts and leaps
And people fall to earth.

Doctor Li Wenliang sees,
Says something
To his boss,
And falls to earth.
His boss, afraid,
Says nothing.

The virus leaps again,
More people fall to earth.

Our doctor sees,
And says something
To his boss,
Who cannot hear
And cannot speak.

JIM LEWIS

The apples grow,
The people eat the apples,
Enjoy the pulp and juice,
And fall to earth.

The season passes,
Apples, uneaten,
Fall to earth,
Tears fall to earth,
And the season ends.

At home,
By candlelight,
We weep.

A MOMENT PLEASE (2020)

(1940) People go to war
To destroy other people,
And we too destroy, trying
To slow this destruction.

I study and question
But do not understand
Why people take from others
Their time and space to live.

(1965) I take the train, it's time for me
To join the movement in the south,
To learn why we are here;
We make time and space for people,
Caring for one another,
Even if some–many–in the south
Do not wish us well.

(1980) We–a girl, a boy–
We find each other,
Find a second chance
To hold each other
And care for others;
It makes a difference,
All the difference
That this world allows;
We see the point.

(2020) For us, this is our evening,
And darkness will bring an end
To our moment in time.

As our moment ends,
I hope, and only hope,
That others have the time and space
To live,
To learn,
To understand,
To see the point,
To care for one another.

MY COUNTRY TIS OF THEE (2020)

"Sweet land of liberty," we sang,
Hopeful and so young,
Knowing it was good for us,
Not knowing what would come.

What comes is always "struggle,"
Writes my friend Don,
Asking his readers to stop,
Look, see, feel–and realize.

"Think through your course,"
Says RBG, planning the way
Forward, opening many doors,
Until her time to leave.

"And keep on pushing,"
Says my friend Harry,
As we ride off to jail;
Too many end up there.

Our leader Bob Moses says,
"Believe the Constitution,"
Promising common good
When we give common effort.

Why must we struggle, plan,
Push and believe? Because
We know the ancient reality:
Good against chaos and evil.

The truth? The truth?
In our sweet land,
Many thirst and hunger,
Finding only ashes.

Can we ignore this knowledge,
Hoping to avoid destruction,
Praying for safety and peace,
Singing of a sweet land?

SERIOUSLY? (2022)

We often ask "who" and "when"
And "what," "where" and "how,"
But not so often "why."

Why did nothing collide
With something
And create matter?
Why did this form stars,
And a planet
With ooze and protein
And then life?

Why did lives
Twist and meet
So that I would
Meet my beloved,
And encourage further life?

Some say, "We have
The answer."
Others say, "We have
No answer."

I say, "We must
Become our answer."

YES, IT IS (2023)

A star forms
And then a planet

Where we now
Find people

Who meet
And find love.

Is it that
Simple?

8

PHOTOS

JIM LEWIS

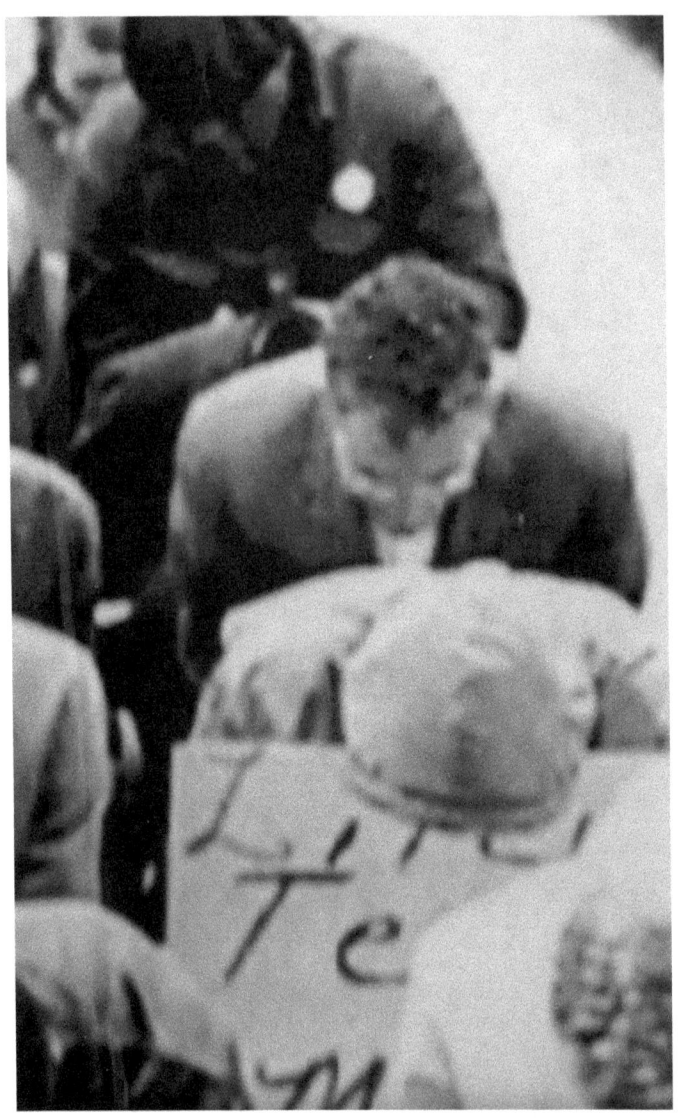

In the picture on the previous page (and the cover), I am under arrest, February 1965, along with fifty friends, peacefully protesting for voting rights at the county courthouse in Magnolia, Mississippi. This picture comes from the files of the Mississippi Sovereignty Commission, the state agency that surveilled (and spied on) the civil rights movement.

The picture on the next page is Wayne Anthony Quin's arrest at the Governor's Mansion in Jackson during the voting rights protest in June 1965. Ms. Quin is there with him (but not in the picture), and she has just told him, "Anthony, don't let that man take your [American] flag."

JIM LEWIS

HERE/NOW

JIM LEWIS

I met John Lewis—twice. For me, just talking with him briefly—among the highlights in my life!

In 2014, John walked into the room, to speak at lunch at a United States Attorney's conference in Washington. Every United States Attorney got up, surrounded him, spoke with him, had a picture with him. For us, he was a beacon of light in the struggle for justice—our struggle. It took us a while to settle back down and listen to what he had to say—and what he had to say was powerful to us all.

That day, I told him that I had three civil rights arrests in Mississippi (in 1965)—these are badges of honor for civil rights workers. I said that I thought he had about 20. I underestimated him: he said it was about 40.

And then, in 2015, John came to the University of Illinois at Springfield, to speak about "March," his graphic novels, providing the people's point of view about the civil rights and voting rights struggles in the 1960s. During dinner in the Public Affairs Center, preceding John's speech, I got a chance to talk with John about our colleagues in the struggle. I have—and treasure—and include—a picture of the two of us talking. After dinner, he spoke to a large and enthusiastic audience in the big auditorium, and he acknowledged me! I will always be touched by this moment of grace.

I loved meeting and talking with him. I love reading about him. He is my hero. He is America's hero, in America's fundamental struggle—to honor its ideals and its purpose.

My daughter Kate's wedding. May 7th, 2016. From left to right: Heather Esme Caramello, Oliver Caramello, Arden Lang, Katherine Lewis, Andrew Thompson, Jim Lewis, Liam Caramello, David Bashwiner.

9

DIRECTIONS

The following is from our daughter Kate.

A Series of Essays by

Kate L. Lewis

*For my mother,
who named me Katherine because she saw my
name as "Kate Lewis" on the cover of my first book.*

*And also because she, by example, has taught her
children not to settle and was smart enough to hold onto a
man like my father.*

CHAPTER 1

We must have a theme, a goal, a purpose in our lives. If you don't know where you're aiming, you don't have a goal. My goal is to live my life in such a way that when I die, someone can say, she cared.
–Mary Kay Ash

It's a typical fall day in central Illinois as I turn the all too familiar corner and come to stop in the driveway. The sky is gray and there is a cool breeze, but it is not all that chilly. The leaves on the old, crooked trees have begun to turn and the street is decked out in fall oranges, reds, and browns. All the other houses on the block are neat–their leaves, freshly raked. Obviously, the landscaping companies made their rounds recently, and the landscaping is pristine, as per usual. And then there's our house. It's a beautiful house with creamy white paint and dark green shutters sitting atop a large hill. It is getting older, though. The paint is starting to peel, showing the need for a little TLC before it will truly fit in on the block of perfect houses with their perfect lawns. Leaves cover the steep drive and lawn, hiding the grass which has seen better days as it barely covers the dirt anymore and has long since turned brown.

I look at my house, my childhood home, and I think about all of the memories of growing up hiding within its walls. The house that looks so disheveled from the street was once a bustling, warm environment perfect for birthday parties, family dinners, and enough memories to last a lifetime. Even more so, I look at the house and take away from it a lesson my father worked hard to teach me and my brother and sister. Just as my house sticks out alongside the perfect, stately houses in the neighborhood, my father sticks out among the other residents, the doctors and the dentists and the busy businessmen. He is not so concerned with the materiality of life. It is as if with the house my father hopes to teach that appearances are deceiving; it's what's on the inside that matters, and inside my house, there was a lot of love.

There were two loving parents who loved their children and, perhaps more importantly, each other--two parents who taught their children the importance of caring for and helping others. My father has dedicated his life to helping the plight of others less fortunate than himself for no other reason than simply wanting to. The house, in a way, embodies the very spirit of my father. He has an aura of simplicity about him, a lack of concern for his physical surroundings, that I have been hard-pressed to find in another individual. Modesty, I suppose.

He drives a dark green 1999 Volkswagen Jetta with a stick shift and manual windows that he bought used from my 33-year-old sister, though he could afford nicer. The car has a tape deck, which I highly doubt he's ever considered using. My dad likes to say that a car needs only to serve its purpose–to transport him to and from work. Nothing more, nothing less. Recently he told me that he wonders if he can even put 6,000 miles a year on a car anymore. Probably not, as life in Springfield is very simple. I think he appreciates simplicity. Weekdays are spent working as a civil litigator for the U.S. Attorney's Office, evenings are spent at meetings for various community causes, and weekends are spent relaxing and going to movies with his wife, my mother. It's a modest existence considering the environment my father grew up in.

My father and I were raised very differently. I am lucky to have two loving, involved parents who worked hard to bestow a certain value system upon their children. And while I don't doubt that my grandparents loved their children, they were certainly more hands-off when it came to parenting. My father will tell you he was essentially raised by two people, George and Elizabeth, who worked in his parents' household for many years taking care of the daily chores and watching out for my dad and his brother. My grandfather owned a very successful sweater and knit business in New York City, and he and my grandmother were very involved in the New York socialite society and much less involved in the lives of their two sons. My grandparents were very wealthy and had live-in help almost their entire married life. My father waited until he went to college and then put as much distance between himself and the land of maids and butlers, Mercedes and BMWs, as possible.

As a senior in college, I feel a certain degree of pressure to find something meaningful to do in the next phase of my life. I think about the distance my dad wanted so badly after school and realize the distance is not only about physical separation, but it is also about leaving behind a lifestyle that he saw as wasteful and counterproductive. I appreciate that his example as a parent and a humanitarian will not force me to seek out the same emotional distance.

On my recent trip home I went to visit my dad at his office. I used to love trips to the office with him when I was little. I would make photocopies of my very small hands and turn them into turkeys for my dad to hang on his filing cabinets. I'm not sure his co-workers appreciated my copy machine dominating art as much as he did, but the office was a veritable playground for a curious child and my father loved showing me around.

Since my most recent visit was on Veterans' Day, the office was closed, and I was saved the joy of passing through security checkpoints. I called my dad and met him in the back alley, entering through the parking garage as though on a behind the scenes tour of the U.S. Attorneys' Office. I waited patiently as my dad punched in his code to open the door to the stairwell. He then proceeded to bounce up the staircase as though it was no trouble as I struggled to keep up with him. He's 65, yet in better shape than I am at 22. He's run the Chicago Marathon for the past few years--just for fun. Even in his running, you can see his relaxed lease on life, his enjoyment of all things simple. He runs marathons because he enjoys them, not to prove anything to anyone. Slow and steady. Just get it done. I imagine that's what goes through his mind as he winds his way through the 26-mile courses. My dad has a knack for simple, straightforward phrases meant to encourage and also for providing vague, yet often helpful advice.

Play hard, have fun. That's what he used to tell my soccer team before our games. Not all of his advice on the soccer field was so prolific. In an attempt to be fair to the other players he coached, I often felt he ignored me. I was the only goalie and there was one week I had a badly sprained wrist, but had yet to go to the doctor–my mom was going to take me after the game. I told my coach, my father, I could not play because my wrist was so swollen I could not move my fingers. For all I knew it was broken. He just looked at me and said, "Well, if you can't catch the ball, just club at it." He smiled and walked away, leaving me speechless. At the time, I was furious. Just club at it? Just keep trying and everything will work out. Looking back I am able to overlook how horrifying I found his advice at the time and appreciate the deeper meaning to what he said. To this day he still tells me to play hard, have fun and just keep moving ahead.

Surprisingly, the civil attorneys are all working the day I go to visit his new office even though it's a federal holiday. They need more attorneys in the division. For this reason, my dad does not decorate his office–out of some sense of protest. He had a bit of a falling out with the head of the office over the issue, so he feels he's making a statement that his presence is not so permanent anymore. I think of it as his own subtle version of the civil disobedience that once was the center of his life. In his old office, he had all sorts of interesting displays. My favorite were probably my hand turkeys, but, as I grew up, I grew to appreciate the copy of the Magna Carta on the wall almost as much. Today the only decoration in his office, aside from the lovely furniture made by federal prisoners with the drawers that randomly fall open, is a small picture frame I sent him this summer when I came home from my internship in Washington, DC. There are two pictures in it, one of our whole family–my mom, my dad, my brother and sister, my brother-in-law, my nephew, and me–and then there's one of just my dad and me.

The new office feels sterile. The bright blue carpet and yellow walls shout U.S. government, while the dark wood furniture seems too fancy standing next to the old, metal filing cabinets that used to be home to my artwork. My dad is neat and organized, something I certainly did not inherit, and his office is businesslike. Come in, work, and leave. It serves its purpose. Nothing more, nothing less. He sees no need for interesting toys or for boasting about his three impressive degrees–one from Yale, one from Duke, and one from the University of Chicago.

I look around and I think about how annoyed my mother gets that my father "plays dumb." He is undeniably brilliant but prefers to not let others in on that secret. He is very modest and avoids telling people too much about the amazing work he has done in his life. He doesn't even like to tell people where he's gone to school, whereas many people would not pass up such an opportunity to brag. He prefers simplicity. Commonality, in a way.

I sit down to interview my dad. He wears hiking boots and an old, woolen, Irish sweater that he's had for as long as I can remember. He rarely matches, wears his pants too short, and often draws criticism for his appearance from my mother and I. We tease him for wearing unblended bifocal glasses, but he finds them practical. He keeps his white hair very short and I've never seen him with facial hair. I just look at him and think about the simplicity and the routine he embodies. There is just no better word than simple to use to describe him.

My dad is a storyteller. When I was little he told me childhood stories at bedtime about the trouble he got into as a young child. My favorite story was one in which my dad and his older brother, my uncle, took a little rowboat down the stream in their backyard to a nearby golf course to collect golf balls. They then sold the golf balls back to the golfers the next day for a small profit. I love his stories about skipping school and piano lessons and all sorts of other childish antics. It's nice to know that a man who has worked so hard for so many years still had a childhood. Play hard, have fun. His wild tales add a hint of humanity that can be so difficult to recognize in our parents sometimes.

As I've grown older, so have the messages of my father's stories. My dad went down to Mississippi twice while he was still in law school and then moved there permanently after he graduated. He was arrested three times during law school because of his strong moral sense of duty. Twice he was arrested for picketing, once spending 12 days in jail while trying to raise enough bail money for everyone to get out, even though he could have bailed himself out the first day. The third time he was technically arrested for swimming in a "closed" park, but in reality, he will tell you it was for swimming with African-Americans in a public park–a real crime in 1960s Mississippi.

As I interview my father, I am continually amazed at how little he takes credit for. The legal and social work he did in Mississippi was unbelievably important in shaping the history of our country, and he will gladly talk about the civil rights movement and about the work that others did. But it is a rare day to get him to sit down and say, "Personally, me, this is what I did." There is a sense of a collective, community involvement that seems foreign in this day and age. He went down to Mississippi because he felt it was the right thing, and an important thing, to do. He lived in houses that had been bombed and in hostile neighborhoods while working to secure constitutional rights for everyone around. It never ceases to amaze me how this man from the suburbs of New York whose parents were wealthy and elitist wound up living in poverty and working for the good of those around him. It shows the cleavage between the way he was raised and the way he lives his life. The distance is not just physical.

After spending the summer in Washington, DC, my first stop in Madison was an interview for another internship. During the interview one of the questions asked of me was who, outside of my family, is my hero. It was an unbelievably difficult question for me to answer. I have never needed to look outside my family for a hero. My father is smart, kind, caring, and dedicated. He gives back to the community and works hard to set an example for those around him without overwhelming people with his accomplishments, often without even mentioning them.

In January there is an annual breakfast in Springfield commemorating the life of Martin Luther King Jr. complete with an often famous guest speaker like Morris Dees, co-founder of the Southern Poverty Law Center. This year they were unable to get their first choice, Senator Barack Obama–rising star of the Democratic Party. Filling in for the Senator will be my father, Jim Lewis. Bernard Malamud once said, "without heroes, we're all plain people and don't know how far we can go." I look to my father and come away with a different message. We are all plain people, but sometimes being the best plain person you can make you a hero. When I graduate in May I will have two options to consider. I can choose to involve myself in my own career and my own life, or I can choose to form my career around being involved in bettering the world for others. My father didn't want to get lost in the dreams of his father by joining the family business and leading a New York socialite's life. My father's dream was to put as much distance, physical, and more importantly otherwise, between himself and his family by becoming a dedicated activist and humanitarian. I, unlike my father, will be lucky if I can get lost in the dreams of my father and make it my own dream to be the kind of person he has raised me, by example, to be.

FIN

www.ingramcontent.com/pod-product-compliance
Lightning Source LLC
LaVergne TN
LVHW011832060526
838200LV00053B/3987